second edition

THE HELPING RELATIONSHIP

PROCESS AND SKILLS

LAWRENCE M. BRAMMER
The University of Washington

PRENTICE-HALL, INC., Englewood Cliffs, New Jersey 07632

Library of Congress Cataloging in Publication Data

BRAMMER, LAWRENCE M

The helping relationship.

(Prentice-Hall series in counseling and human development)

Bibliography: p.

Includes index.

1. Counseling. 2. Helping behavior. I. Title.

BF637.C6B676 1979 361.3'2'019 78-12019

ISBN 0-13-386250-X (p)

ISBN 0-13-386268-2 (c)

PRENTICE-HALL SERIES IN COUNSELING AND HUMAN DEVELOPMENT

Norman R. Stewart, Consulting Editor

Printed in the United States of America

10 9 8 7 6 5 4 3 2

Editorial/production supervision and interior design by Joan L. Lee
Cover design by Judith Winthrop
Cover design art by Kenneth M. Davis
Manufacturing buyers: Gordon Osbourne and John Hall

PRENTICE-HALL INTERNATIONAL, INC., *London*
PRENTICE-HALL OF AUSTRALIA PTY. LIMITED, *Sydney*
PRENTICE-HALL OF CANADA, LTD., *Toronto*
PRENTICE-HALL OF INDIA PRIVATE LIMITED, *New Delhi*
PRENTICE-HALL OF JAPAN, INC., *Tokyo*
PRENTICE-HALL OF SOUTHEAST ASIA PTE. LTD., *Singapore*
WHITEHALL BOOKS LIMITED, *Wellington, New Zealand*

CONTENTS

TWO CHARACTERISTICS OF HELPERS, *22*

THREE THE HELPING PROCESS, *44*

FOUR HELPING SKILLS FOR UNDERSTANDING, *67*

FIVE HELPING SKILLS FOR COMFORT AND CRISIS UTILIZATION, *100*

SIX HELPING SKILLS FOR POSITIVE ACTION AND BEHAVIOR CHANGE, *126*

Introduction

People want to help one another. The basic purposes of this book are to describe this helping process and to provide a road map for interested people helpers to guide them in thinking through some relevant principles, skills, and research.

Although great progress has been made in material technology, we are still in the dark ages of human relations and exploration of human potentiality. Now that humans have substantial mastery over nature, we are searching for better ways to manage ourselves. We want improvements in our relationships so that we can be better parents, spouses, and friends. The growing popularity of applied psychology books, growth centers, parent education, encounter groups, and voluntary services are ripples on the surface of our profound desire to help others. Now that the basic survival needs of most people are satisfied they are searching for deeper meanings in their lives through service to others.

Our basic problem is how to apply the existing vast resources for helping to the equally vast human problems plaguing our society. We cannot depend solely on helping specialists and human relations experts to close this large gap. A helping commitment must be encouraged and helping skills must be widely dispersed in the population until human satisfactions and better social organization make formal helping, as we now know it, unnecessary. One scenario is the possibility that we all become helpers, facilitating one another's development and search for happiness.

While there is a need for specialists trained to cope with the complexities of human problems, most human needs can be (and have been) met by nonspecialist helpers. This book is written mainly for such nonspecialists who want a framework in which to view their helping functions, and for those who wish to join classes studying helping functions and skills in a systematic manner. Thus, people who work as generalists in counseling, group leadership, child care, youth work, teaching, nursing, rehabilitation, employment, police work, community relations, mental health, parent education, crisis centers, or church work will, it is hoped, apply these principles and techniques to their work settings. In addition to these special helpers it appears that about half of all jobs involve some human contact service, and this proportion is likely to increase. Therefore, all people with personal contact positions will find this book useful.

Persons in consulting and instructional roles in community agencies and educational institutions will be able to use this book for in-service education on helping skills and human relations. Those persons following a programmed learning approach to human relations, communication skills, or counseling will find this text a useful framework for their skills training.

This book focuses on helping normal individuals to function at a higher level. It is not a book on psychotherapy and the pathology of human interaction. I emphasize basic communication skill improvement, since a fundamental problem in all human relations is our difficulty in reaching one another successfully.

The two keys to the helping process are the helper as a person and his or her skills. This book concentrates on the helper's task of becoming a more aware and effective person. He or she is first of all a human being, and secondly, a helping instrument in the form of parent, teacher, counselor, adviser, interviewer, or friend. The second key the helper needs is precise skills to realize the outcomes people desire. These skills are presented in the categories of understanding, comfort, and action.

I have attempted to present in simple form many principles and skills gleaned from twenty years as teacher, counselor, and behavioral science researcher in the people-helping realm. Yet I recognize that the helping function can be complex and controversial. We possess no neat body of valid knowledge about the helping process, but we have a good start. This book is an effort to describe this evolving process and to consider the helping process in light of changing social needs and diverse definitions of helpfulness.

I have minimized citations, quotations, and technical terms in my quest for clarity and simplicity and have included, reluctantly, only a sampling of the extensive literature from the helping professions. Suggestions for further study are included with each chapter. The appendix includes three brief learning packages as samples of what students or instructors can construct for themselves. This text is not intended as a collection of systematic skills exercises.

I wish to acknowledge the helpfulness of Mrs. Winifred Raymond, Mrs. Jean Swindlehurst, and Mrs. Sharon Roberts in the preparation of the manuscript. I am deeply grateful to Dr. Allen Ivey and Mrs. Margaret Pratt for their encouragement and helpful suggestions. Thanks also to my wife, Marian, for her patience during this writing and her cogent suggestions from her experience as a teacher and parent.

ONE

HELPING: WHAT DOES IT MEAN?

This is a book about people helping other people to grow toward their personal goals and to strengthen their capacities for coping with life. Few of us achieve our growth goals or solve our personal problems alone. We need other people in some kind of helping relationship to us, but what does this need imply for helpers and the helped?

WHAT IS YOUR VIEW OF HELPING?

Think about your own view of what helping means and examine your motives for helping people. My principal goal in this chapter is to assist you in thinking through and in extending your views of the helping process, because you must develop a style of help that is comfortable and effective for you. Take some time for the following activities.

1. What does it mean to be a helper? Picture yourself helping another person. Imagine a specific setting. What are you doing? What are you saying? What are you feeling? How is the other person responding? Make a list of the behaviors you regard as helpful.

2. Relax; then try to recall people who have helped you. What were the behaviors and personal qualities that made them helpful people? How did you feel about their actions? What did you infer about their attitudes? List their helpful behaviors.

3. Ask close friends or relatives to describe incidents when your behavior was helpful to them. List their descriptive words and phrases.

4. Compare your three lists of your concept of a helper, your perceptions of others as helpers, and other people's views of you as a helper. Keep them for later comparison with lists in the following chapters.

5. Spend time thinking of all the phrases and feelings that occur to you when you consider the questions: Why do I want to be a helper? Whom do I want to help? What do I get out of the helping process? How do I want to be perceived by those I intend to help? How do I feel about what comes to my awareness during this activity? Write a descriptive paragraph about yourself as a helper before these thoughts and feelings disappear.

If possible, share these ideas and lists with others doing the same activities. Sharing and receiving reactions helps to clarify and amplify one's ideas and feelings about such a personal topic. It is difficult to be honest about motives for helping others. Compare your lists with the discussion of illustrative motives in later paragraphs and in chapter 2.

No doubt you found that *helping* is a difficult process to describe because it has such individualized meanings. It is necessary to understand these numerous meanings of help, however, because all of us have work, community, or family responsibilities that demand helping relationships.

A further complication in definition is that *help* means different things to people in various subcultures. The idea of helping, in the sense of counseling, is largely an American white middle-class phenomenon. In most other cultures, helping functions are unobtrusive acts performed in informal settings, such as families. *La familia* brings up immediate meanings of loyalty and service, for example, when mentioned in Spanish-speaking groups. One's concept of helpfulness must be placed in a cultural framework and must take into account the special meanings and unique language associated with it by various racial, ethnic, and sex groupings.

This chapter explores these meanings further, and the following chapter examines the characteristics of effective helpers. A detailed presentation of helping skills and action principles is made in the remaining chapters. Theories about helping processes and basic helping relationships conclude this book.

For purposes of this book the helping person will be designated as the *helper*, and the helped as the *helpee*. While awkward terms, they serve as more generalized designations for counselor-counselee, worker-client, therapist-patient, parent-child, teacher-pupil, and interviewer-interviewee commonly used in public agency and private practice settings. My underlying assumption is that the basic interpersonal communication processes implied by these specialized helping relationships are similar.

Some Goals and Viewpoints

It follows from our discussion that helpers need to know:

1. What helping means—its potentials and pitfalls;
2. What steps both helper and helpee need to take to reach their goals;
3. What skills and facilitative characteristics helpers and helpees need;
4. How helpers learn and apply the required skills; and
5. How helpers improve their helping services—how they develop a theory and research base.

I will begin with some of my ideas about helpers and helping as building blocks for the remaining chapters. These generalizations are primarily value statements and assumptions with varying degrees of demonstrated validity, because very few statements about helping are universally true. Some statements are based on my experience, and some are verified generalizations from behavioral science research.

Outcomes You Can Expect

By studying this chapter you should be able to: (1) state your own view of helping and why you want to help; (2) list three sources of personal gain to the helper from engaging in the helping process; (3) identify the basic points of view of this book; (4) describe the essential nature of the helping process in terms of need fulfillment and responsible independence; (5) list three arguments that support, and three that refute, the professional and nonprofessional approaches to helping; (6) describe and illustrate self-help, peer, cross-age, and community helper projects; and (7) list twelve basic helping skills.

The Helping Process

Figure 1 shows the main elements of the helping process: the helper's personality, combined with specific skills, produce growth conditions that lead to definite outcomes important to the person, the helper, and society in general. Whereas helper personality and skills constitute the basic ingredients of the process, specialists are a third element that broadens the helpers' awareness and that realizes their helping potential. Specialists investigate the recorded experience of other helpers as well as the contributions of the behavioral sciences, and they formulate helping theories of their own. The more specialized helpers also ask questions about the value of their helping services and learn research skills with which to answer those questions.

Universality of Help

Helping is a function of *all* concerned human beings and is *not* limited to professional helpers. One of the significant developments in our specialized technical society was the professionalization of the helping process. Professional helpers realized that they could not be all things to all people, and specialization resulted from the professionals' sincere desires to maximize the delivery of quality helping services. They also wanted to protect the unsuspecting public from unscrupulous or ignorant helpers who charged fees. The consequence of this development was to assign helping functions by custom and law to specialists! Another result of professionalization was a whole substructure of special terminology, organizations, credentials, status levels, and ethical codes. As we shall see later in this chapter, these developments in the helping professions have created some agonizing public issues surrounding credentialling, legality, competence, ethics, funding, and service delivery.

One purpose of this book is to make some of the learnings of helping specialists more available to persons not having specialist responsibilities, and to encourage more widespread volunteer helping behaviors. Specialist helpers are far too few to make a strong impact, and it is

Figure 1. The Helping Process

Personality of Helper	+	*Helping Skills*	→	*Growth-Facilitating Conditions*	→	*Specific Outcomes*
Traits		For understanding		Trust		For the person
Attitudes		For comfort		Respect		For society
Values		For action		Freedom		For the helper

a social tragedy to restrict basic helping functions to a few specialists. This effort is not designed to minimize the contribution of specialists nor to disparage the skill and knowledge acquired in years of research, study, and practice. Meeting the health, psychological, and spiritual needs of dysfunctional people in our increasingly dehumanized society is so complicated and demanding that specialists will continue to be needed. But these specialists should be employed only when their unique knowledge can be used effectively. Overreliance on a specialized approach often ignores and fragments the needs of the whole person.

The overlapping functions of helping specialties is another confusing reality, since there are many labels for substantially the same helping process. The process, furthermore, has much in common with friendship. Schofield (1964) made an elaborate case that helping specialists offer a substantial amount of friendship to their clients. The irony is that these clients pay for friendship they should obtain in normal processes of living. It is a severe indictment of our culture that people must purchase friendship.

Facilitating Helpee Growth

Helping another human being is basically a process of enabling that person to grow in the directions that person chooses, to solve problems, and to face crises. This process assumes the helpee is aware of alternatives and is willing to take responsibility for acting on an alternative. Helping involves facilitating awareness of such alternatives and assessing readiness to act. Help, however, should be defined mainly by the helpees, who select the goals of their own growth, and who also determine whether they want help at all. To avoid feeling patronized helpees define desired help on their own terms and fulfill their own needs. They may, for example, ask for information, or for assistance in making a decision, solving a problem, or expressing their feelings. We need to be aware, though, that helpees seldom admit directly that they want help, because it is difficult to admit having a problem one cannot solve on one's own. Even when helpees admit to themselves that they have problems, the degree of trust they feel will determine the extent of their sharing with a helping person. In any case, this view of helping assumes that helpees know their needs.

This voluntary quality of the helping process is a crucial point since many persons wanting to help others actually seek to meet their own unrecognized needs. Some helpers, for example, *need* "victims"; the helpers may maintain relationships to satisfy their own affiliative or dominance needs and may even continue their relationship longer than necessary in order to feel needed. Doing anything for other people without their initiative and consent frequently is manipulative and often is destructive. Even when the help is solicited and given with the best of human motives it may have an unplanned detrimental effect on the helpee. The reason is partly that persons being helped experience a loss of self-esteem. Although appearing outwardly grateful, they may interpret the gift or act of help as a message that they are incompetent. This interpretation is accompanied by feelings of dependency, helplessness, inferiority, or inadequacy. They say to themselves, for example, "Receiving this help makes me feel as if I can't take care of myself; I don't like leaning on somebody else." Such feelings often turn quickly to resentment or guilt, especially for informal help. These common self-protective reactions are one reason the helping process has such unpredictable outcomes and why helping actions are often resented.

The underlying issue of this section is the extent to which one should or can take responsibility for another person. Helpers vary over the full spectrum of responsibility from feeling a deep sense of human obligation to meet the needs of others to a view that others are totally responsible for their own experience and need fulfillment. The former group believes strongly that "I am my brother's keeper." The latter group claims that giving help perpetuates dependency and immaturity in the helpee. Help may vary over the entire range depending on the circumstances. Generally the aim is to make the helpee self-sufficient; thus, bids for help and our inclinations to be helpful need to be scrutinized with this goal in the foreground. There are times, though, when the human thing to do is to give total support to another without regard to dependency problems. Important questions for helpers to ask themselves are, What is this person's capacity for responsible independence and self-support at this time? How can I be supportive without reinforcing this person's dependency? What needs and rationalization prompt my own desires to be helpful at this time? Chapter 2 contains a more detailed discussion of helping motives and rewards for the helper.

A dilemma facing helpers is, help for whom—the person, the agency, or society? If helpers indicate by behavior or attitude to their helpees that they are looking after the agency's interests only, they incur wrath and rejection. On the other hand, helpers cannot always support their helpees with the attitude that society or the agency is the enemy. The most helpful stance is to assist helpees to see how their present behavior is shaped by their environment. The aim is understanding, not blame.

A large amount of research evidence supports the claim that ostensibly helping relationships may be destructive, or at least nonconsequential, for normal people, and for those pathologically inclined as well. This research has been surveyed by Carkhuff (1969) who concluded that the observed constructive results of the helping process were cancelled out by deteriorative results when the data were lumped together. When the average gains of the helped groups were compared with averages of the non-helped control groups, there were no significant differences. It is the difficult task of all serious people-helpers to look critically at their own helping behavior and the consequences for helpees' behavior to determine if their help was effective, ineffective, or destructive.

The act of helping people with the presumed goal of doing something for them, or changing them in some way, has an arrogant quality also. This implication of superiority raises hostile feelings in the helpee because the act presumes that the helper is wiser, more competent, and more powerful than the helpee. Although these conditions may be true, as judged by external observers, the motive for help and the nature of the helping task as perceived by the helper must be made clear to the receiver.

The principle that helpees must initiate the help request is confusing in another way. Must they always ask for help in words? A hurting child, for example, often cannot state clearly what he or she wants verbally, but expressions and body tension may be saying "Help me!" Our inferences from reading these behaviors could be wrong, but the only way we can know is to respond, and then be alert to the reactions. A similar and unusual situation is the attempted suicide, which may be interpreted as a desperate call for help. The idea that help must always be requested in verbal terms certainly can be carried to extremes, particularly in situations that present danger to the person.

The aim of all help is *self-help* and eventual self-sufficiency. I have emphasized that much of our growth is the result of self-help and self-searching, rather than a result of something done to or for us. Our needs for autonomy and self-actualization are strong, yet sometimes they are subdued temporarily by life experiences. These needs must be respected and strengthened for psychological survival, at least, and self-actualization, at best.

A further assumption I wish to include here is that each of us behaves in a competent and trustworthy manner if given the freedom and encouragement to do so. Sometimes this confidence is shaken when working with people who have been hurt deeply by life and who behave consequently in an irresponsible and untrustworthy manner. We must communicate to helpees our confidence and trust in their ability to move toward goals best for them and for society. In this discussion of helping I have stressed the significance of helpee *responsibility* for such goals and self-determined growth because, in my view, this is the main purpose of helping. To assist helpees in carrying out their responsibilities we provide them with life management skills whereby they can help themselves. Improving interpersonal communication skills alone can have a dramatic positive effect on other areas of living also (Pierce and Drasgow 1969; Authier, Gustafson, Guerney, and Kasdorf 1975).

We, as helpers, also must assume some responsibility for creating conditions of trust whereby helpees can respond in a trusting manner and help themselves. Helpers do this through the *process,* a term which refers largely to their methods for bringing about helpee outcomes. These outcomes are realized through managing the environment, providing conditions for understanding and comfort, and modeling trusting behaviors. A trusting approach means that helpers view their task as facilitating and supporting, rather than as teaching or persuading. Helpers who are open and honest about their own ideas and feelings tend to be perceived as trustworthy by their helpees. Consistent behaviors that show caring and are clearly in the helpees' best interests also inspire trust.

While we are concerned with the helpee's inner feelings, values, and goals, we must be alert also to the impact on the helpee of other people and of the physical environment. One implication of this view is that the helper needs to understand the special life circumstances of helpees and to get out of the office or agency sanctuary. Another implication is that a helpee is anyone who brings a matter to the helper's attention—a teacher or parent concerned about a child or a supervisor about an employee, as well as people who ask for help directly for themselves.

Helping by Agreement

As a helping relationship develops, an important consideration is the nature of the agreement or "contract" between the helper and helpee. When help is requested outside of a friendship setting, it is important that the terms and conditions of the help be agreed on early. Helpers get themselves into difficult situations in which they try more than they can capably or ethically deliver when the expectations of both parties are not explored and agreed on. How this is done formally and informally will be described in chapters 3 and 6 under "structuring" and "contracting." An example of a working agreement in formal helping settings is to tell helpees, "I agree to meet with you for an hour a week for about three weeks to work on this concern; you will come here to work with me and will do some work outside our interviews.

We will decide in three weeks how we will proceed." Sometimes this simple agreement is formalized into a more detailed contract with written terms about what each will do.

The nature of the agreement should imply a growth contract, that helpees will try to change under their own initiative, with minimal helper assistance. If helpers become preoccupied with the notion that *they* must help other people, that *they* must produce some change, then helpees have a demanding hold on them which could be very manipulative and destructive for all. Disturbed people with persistent adjustment problems often seek out such helping types, but they only frustrate their helpers' efforts. Helpees in this instance are looking for something very idealistic or are demanding that something specific and unrealistic be given to them. Helpers who falls into this trap reinforce the "helpless" or "sick" games of helpees, thus preventing them from taking responsibility for helping themselves. This topic will be expanded in later sections, but it is important for our introductory purposes here to realize the serious and complex nature of the commitment one makes as a helper.

Meeting Helpee Needs

Help consists of providing conditions for helpees to meet their needs. Help varies (across a spectrum) from strong physical intervention, such as averting a suicide, to subtle emotional support, such as counseling for finding a new job. The kind and amount of help given depends on the helpee's needs at the time. These human needs can be classified in various ways. A scheme that makes most sense to me was developed by Maslow (1962), and I offer it here as an example of a need system to understand the nature of help. Maslow arranges needs in a complex interrelated hierarchy of five levels according to their primacy in human existence. These five levels are *physiological, safety, love and belonging, self-esteem,* and *self-actualization.*

Physiological needs for sustaining life are so primary that until people have enough to eat, for example, any other form of helping is irrelevant. These physical needs are self-preservative and reproductive. Thus, helping means meeting a basic physical need such as food or clothing. For purposes of this book, however, helping processes will be restricted largely to acts of counseling, consulting, teaching, or facilitating satisfaction of psychosocial needs to be described below.

A second level of needs is for psychological safety, or security. We want to feel secure in our person. We want to know that our future is predictable. We are suspicious of change, and we want to reduce the tension from conflict, cruelty, injustice, and uncertainty.

The third level is love and belonging. We want to feel part of some enduring group where we are accepted, wanted, loved, and respected. When these conditions are reasonably satisfied, we can give love and respect to others. We then are able to show others we care and are interested in being helpful. If these love and belonging needs are not fulfilled in ourselves, we tend to resort to numerous self-defeating or attention-getting behaviors, such as suspicion and aggression.

The fourth need level in Maslow's system is for achievement of self-esteem. To feel good about ourselves we need to be liked and regarded as valuable and competent by others. As we grow in awareness of our self-worth and get more in touch with our deeper needs, feelings, and values, we depend less on others' judgments of our worth. The key implication here for the helping process is to find ways for people to think well of themselves, to believe in their competence and worth, through relationships with us.

It is difficult to define or describe the fifth need level, which functions best when the four lower levels of need are in process of being satisfied. This self-actualizing level is a striving for self-development, integration, autonomy, stimulation, and challenge. It involves reaching out, often in risky ways, to move to higher levels of satisfaction and growth.

The first four levels Maslow calls "D," or deficiency, needs. This person strives for fulfillment of a felt deficit, such as hunger, desire for love, or need for social response. Gratification brings a kind of calm and satisfaction for a time; satisfaction averts the usual physical and emotional problems that deficits bring about. Yet what most people feel quickly after gratification is a vague craving for "something more." Maslow classified these needs for becoming more integrated, challenged, and individualized "B," or being, needs, to maintain a sense of high-level humanness and self-actualization (the fifth level). People must do what they feel they can—paint, write, love, or serve.

The significance of need theory for understanding the helping process is that many requests for help come in the form of meeting deficiencies in needs for love, security, self-respect, or social stimulation. We must help people fulfill their basic physical and psychological needs before they can achieve higher levels of being and achievement. If their basic needs are met, people will be less inclined to satisfy their deficiencies through crime, violence, and emotional distress.

It is paradoxical, however, that this self-actualization need is achieved largely through help from other people. Yet Maslow's model of self-actualized persons was characterized by independence and self-sufficiency to accomplish these states with their own initiative and resources. In other words, it is possible that helping relationships beyond a certain point might retard the helpee's independence and self-esteem. This paradox translates into the assertion that the most helpful thing we can do for other people is to "help them help themselves" by creating the conditions that release their powerful growth tendencies and abilities to use their own resources. These growth conditions are the cumulative effect of the helper exhibiting many of the traits described in chapter 2. Helper values such as prizing and encouraging the freedom and individuality of others as well as having positive regard for helpees are especially potent.

It is difficult for the helper to determine when helpees are concerned about some basic need satisfaction and when they are asking for help with their dimly perceived strivings for more creativity, autonomy, integration, or achievement. Helpees often have difficulty expressing their wants, since all they experience is feelings of dissatisfaction with themselves, their status, or their behavior. They are aware only that they want something more than satisfaction of their appetites.

In the process of exploring possibilities for their becoming more self-actualized, "becoming" persons discover that their moment-to-moment satisfactions are occasionally punctuated with "peak experiences." These are feelings described by Maslow as transient states of being, characterized by joy, delight, or even ecstacy. Thus, helping can be construed as a process of assisting helpees toward higher levels of self-actualization and the joyful realization of their unused possibilities.

Helping can be a process also of achieving awareness of the conflict between the attractions of safety and comfort, on the one hand, and the risks and magnetism of growth on the other. Each condition has its delight and repugnance.

Science and Art of Helping

Helping is both science and art. The science portion involves elaborate research and theory on helping, mainly from the behavioral sciences, whereas the artistic aspects of helping refer more to the intuitive and feeling elements of interpersonal relationships that are based largely in the humanities and creative arts. The scientific aspect is concerned with descriptive data, predictions, and generalizations about behavior. Nonprofessional helpers, although lacking this sophisticated behavioral science background and skill training, often can apply helping principles in their intuitive artistic fashion. One implication of the research to be cited below is to select persons as helpers who already possess these artful qualities, and then quickly and systematically give them basic helping skills and behavior concepts. I will emphasize this dual behavioral science and artistic approach to the helping function throughout this book.

Structured and Unstructured Helping

Helping affiliations can be classified into various levels, from formal and structured to informal and unstructured as illustrated below.

Structured

Professional helpers. (Examples: social workers, ministers, psychologists, teachers, school counselors, physicians, nurses, psychiatrists, legal counselors with specialized training and legal responsibility.)

Paraprofessional helpers. (Examples: trained interviewers, receptionists, aides in mental health and rehabilitation, and persons in correctional, educational, employment, and social agency settings.)

Volunteers. (Nonpaid persons with short-term training in basic helping skills and agency orientation.)

Unstructured

Friendships. (Informal, mutual, and unstructured helping relationships over time.)

Family. (Informal mutual helping system, interdependent in variable degrees.)

Community and general human concern. (Informal, unstructured, ad hoc helping acts to alleviate danger, suffering, or deprivation.)

The focus of this book is on the more structured forms of helping. Yet, it is striking to realize that formalized helping relationships in the form of counseling, treatment, ministering, or psychotherapy have characteristics in common with all effective human relating.

Professionals and Paraprofessionals

One of the main reasons for the increased employment of helpers outside of traditional professions is that data from some investigators, such as Carkhuff (1968), suggest that the effectiveness of professional helpers is much less than claimed or believed. These findings, coupled with data on the speed with which productive helping skills can be learned by nonprofessionals, suggest the desirability and feasibility of involving more such persons in the formal helping process. Rioch (1966) and Carkhuff and Truax (1965), for example, demonstrated the effectiveness of training nonprofessional adult helpers in mental health settings.

I would like to point out, as an editorial aside, that we have learned to depend heavily on experts in the helping professions, and we have allowed them to appropriate normal growth-producing processes into the mystical and sometimes exclusive domain of a professional guild. Too often elaborate professional entrance rituals are associated with a "divine right" to practice. This attitude leads frequently to interprofessional rivalries and jurisdictional disputes, such as those between psychiatrists and psychologists. This condition often puts guild welfare ahead of personal service. Laws have been passed, for example, that define psychotherapy and counseling and that designate who can perform these functions as a service to the public. Although designed to protect the public from unscrupulous fee-charging helpers, such laws also tend to constrict helping services to the more knowing and affluent people. This is a dilemma that we must resolve soon in our society.

Helping persons without the usual credentials sometimes are regarded as a threat to those with certificates and degrees in a helping specialty. Yet, it is sheer social folly not to utilize the untapped resources of helping talent in the nonprofessional population. Guerney (1969) makes a persuasive case for the use of nonspecialist helpers to meet manpower needs, particularly in services to children. Such nonspecialists, often called paraprofessionals or "indigenous nonprofessionals," are widely used in service delivery in all kinds of helping agencies (Steenland 1973). Furthermore, there are abundant roles in training, research, and consultation for those helpers with more extensive and specialized skills and knowledge. The important consideration is who can be the best "significant other" to the person with emotional-social problems, and who can supplement parents and teachers with close sustained relationships to children. Many professional helpers, for example, depend on verbal means of treatment help and thus limit their effectiveness to verbally facile educated middle and upper social class people. Numerous persons needing help find direct nonverbal communication means more helpful.

Time, too, affects the helping process. Usually the professional spends little time with a helpee compared to others significant in his or her life. If these significant others received training in basic helping skills to supplement whatever natural helping attitudes they had acquired in normal development, they might make an even greater impact on the helpee than a whole clinic of professionals. The key question is, who can serve the helpee most effectively? We must define effectiveness more precisely, however, before we can answer.

Our society needs a "third mental health revolution," described by Hobbs (1964) as an extensive and early preventive effort, coupled with an expanded human potential movement, to help people move to higher levels of functioning. To facilitate this revolution we will need masses of helping persons who are more available than the usual professional specialists, and who have confidence that we can change our culture from one that exploits to one that serves its people.

To bring about Hobbs' "revolution" and Leonard's "transformation" (Leonard 1973), a massive educational effort aimed toward teaching skills in human relations, interpersonal communication, human development, and self-care is needed. Ivey and Weinstein (1970) and Mosher and Sprinthall (1971) describe "psychological education" as an effort to make the specialized skills and knowledge of helping specialists more widely known and used by the general population. They make a strong case for shifting more helping efforts of counselors from direct service of helpees to psychological education of helpers.

Many people have natural capacities to be helpful because of their fortunate life experiences. They have the intellectual capacity to understand and nurture such natural helping characteristics so that they can be even more helpful to others. I believe that many of these persons, furthermore, have the capacity for insight into the destructive potential of these natural helping processes if they are not used for the benefit of the helpee. It is necessary, for example, that helpers become aware of their power over others when they are intending to help, and of how easy it is to abuse that power unknowingly.

In spite of their many advantages, nonprofessional helpers are subject to the same tendencies as professionals to distort their views of helpees or to project their own problems on the helpees. Furthermore, nonprofessionals are less likely to be aware of these possible distortions as professionals who go through extensive supervision and training. The nonprofessional helper also is likely to pick up "contagious" feelings from the helpee, whereas the professional has learned a kind of professional "distance" to counter this tendency. Both of these limitations can be greatly reduced if the helper seeks or is assigned a supervising person skilled in promoting a necessary self-awareness.

Although this tendency toward emotional overinvolvement can be a limitation, it has the potential for strength as well. For example, the tendency for nonprofessionals to immerse themselves deeply in the emotional life of the helpee can facilitate helpee growth more than the tendency of professionals to remain detached. This complicated issue will be explored further in chapter 3.

In this era of accountability for outcomes, supervision from a professional can transmit an awareness of responsibility for what happens to helpees. This ethical commitment to helpees and a sense of social responsibility are significant aspects of helper training.

I have been comparing the specialist professional with the generalist nonprofessional helper, but classifying helpers into these two categories is artificial and limiting. Professional helpers earn their hard-won labels through completing a prescribed program of training, meeting competency examination and licensing requirements, adhering to prescribed ethical standards, and being accountable for the outcomes of their help. *Paraprofessional,* on the other hand, is a term applied to persons with some of the skills and natural helping talents of the professional. They usually work directly with helpees under the professional's supervision for training and agency accountability. A more descriptive term without the lower status implications of paraprofessional is needed, but this is the designation being used for the present time.

In agencies that use both professional and paraprofessional staff, issues soon arise over distinctive roles, client responsibility, essential qualifications, pay scales, and evaluation of helping effectiveness. Arguments and research around these issues could go on endlessly, but effective solutions can come about only with honest staff discussions of their respective strengths, limitations, and contributions. Each may be effective in meeting certain helpee needs and expectations, yet both helper groups are handicapped by helpee expectations that exceed current knowledge about the helping process. The basic problem, then, is matching helper self-perceptions of qualifications with helpee and agency expectations.

A second problem is determining and evaluating the complex variables that are assumed to be related to helping effectiveness. These variables are basic empathic qualities, knowledge of research and theory, skill performance, legal and ethical accountability to helpees and agencies, special knowledge from training or experience, and evaluation of competence by peers and professional associations.

Opinions in psychology and social work literature are divided between those who feel that paraprofessional helpers should function under close supervision as support and administrative personnel, on the one hand, and as independent helping persons on the other. By now it should be clear that my opinions support the latter view, providing due attention is given to the performance issues cited above.

Community, Peer, and Cross-Age Helping

Additional applications of the informal helping principle are peer and cross-age helpers, people of similar ages, or persons with similar problems, who help others of comparable age or condition. An example is

Alcoholics Anonymous, where former problem drinkers help those wishing to reduce their drinking. Numerous youth drug therapy and unwed mother programs use peers who experienced and solved similar problems as the helping agents. The New York Haryou program (*Youth in the Ghetto* 1964), for example, is based on the idea that people not only meet their own needs to be helpful, but also solve their own problems while helping others. The "Samaritans" is a movement originating in Great Britain, consisting of volunteer unpaid helpers available at all hours to assist the lonely, distraught, and confused people in urban communities. They apply a kind of "first aid" at the time when people need help most. The "Fish" program in the United States, which is organized largely around churches, has similar on-the-spot helping services. Renewed concern about neighborhoods in America is providing additional opportunities for informal helping. In the Netherlands an extensive government sponsored program, translated as "neighborship," is under way to reinstate attitudes and structures of neighborliness once common in more agrarian societies. Most distressed people are not "sick" in a medical sense, but ignorant, deprived, deficient, or abandoned by the community. It is a blot on our humanity that we cannot look after one another more effectively. The helping groups cited above are examples of progress made toward community solutions of these human problems.

In the educational setting the practice of pupils helping other pupils of the same or younger age is increasing. Several studies verify the utility of this method, such as those reported by Hawkinshire (1963). Here fourth graders with reading problems, for example, were assisted by sixth graders also having reading difficulties. While the fourth graders were helped to read significantly better, the helping process greatly enhanced the sixth graders' reading skills. Serving as a teacher-helper, therefore, holds great promise for helping others as well as for acquiring formal helping skills and knowledge to use in many contexts.

Varenhorst and Hamburg (1971, 1972) report the design and evaluation of a program to train youth from seventh through twelfth grades in helping skills for fellow students. These volunteers were given information about youth problems and referral resources along with training in interpersonal skills. The evaluation indicated that this program was very effective in helping students with normal emotional and developmental problems. Dougherty and Dyal's review of peer counseling (1976) revealed the extensive and effective use of peer helpers in the elementary school setting.

Students at the adult level can become effective peer helpers also, as indicated in a community college study by Pyle and Snyder (1971). These students were judged to be very effective in helping fellow students with a small amount of support during the difficult transition to college life, handling dependency and autonomy issues, learning how to learn, and making curricular choices. Those students from ethnic minority backgrounds were helped especially by those who understood their background and problems of adjustment. As in other studies, a significant by-product was the personal growth of the student helpers.

It may be that persistent social problems can be alleviated by peer help also. In many major cities, for example, parents show great concern over busing children to achieve racial balance and to equalize educational opportunity. One of the more covert reasons for this concern is that many parents feel their children will be held back if mixed with children of deprived educational backgrounds. If the peer helper principle could be put into practice, both the accelerated and the less able pupils may benefit from a diverse classroom.

Perhaps children can be helped more by helping others than by following adult models or listening to others who are vastly superior to themselves. Although much work needs to be done on the usefulness of peer-helping relationships, enough is known to stimulate us to explore this helping resource more vigorously. A convincing rationale for use of young peer helpers has been given by Bruner (1972). He regards the intermediate generation of teenagers and youth as new role bearers or models to bridge the gap between generations and to help youth and children enter the adult world. Bruner thinks these young role models should be given more responsibility for teaching the younger, less experienced children because they are key linkages between generations in periods of rapid change. This process could become an endless chain of helping, with the helped becoming helpers of others. The possibilities of peer-helper effectiveness in education, rehabilitation, mental health, corrections, and poverty programs are vast indeed.

Self-Help Groups

There has been little research on why self-help groups are so effective in changing individual behavior. Hurvitz (1970) studied many groups as a participant-observer and concluded that much of their effectiveness was due to peer relationship among helpers and helped, inspirational methods, explicit goals, fellowship, and a variety of helping procedures. Hurvitz sees these self-help efforts as more effective in many cases than professional psychotherapy. Self-help groups use many sources of help that are outside conventional helping methods. They depend heavily on charismatic leaders and often develop a religious or cultish atmosphere with demanding obedience to an authority.

Another type of self-help group is spreading rapidly in America. While the groups cited above are organized around a specific need to change self-destructive behavior such as alcoholism, hard drug abuse, or overeating, these groups are developed by people already functioning reasonably well in society, but who want to grow to higher levels of effectiveness. The groups are organized informally for purposes of spiritual and psychological growth, social enhancement, and mutual support in times of crisis. Such functions, formerly supplied by the extended family or small church community, are now largely absent from the impersonal urban scene. I predict that this self-help movement will become a strong trend in our urban centers.

Helpers Gain Too

Helpers change in the process, too, and as shown by the preceding evidence and discussion of peer helpers, they can receive as much or more than the helped. As a result of being asked to help, the helper's status is increased and his or her self-image is strengthened. Positive self-regard increases as a result of helping another person through giving rather than taking. Increased confidence in one's own psychological well-being comes from the awareness that "I must be O.K. if I can help others in need." The helping process, furthermore, takes people out of themselves and into the perceptual world of the others, thus diminishing concern with their own problems; sharing feelings often results in strong mutual satisfactions for both people. We need to recognize this strong need to be helpful to others and to provide more opportunities for volunteers to train and serve. The National Training Laboratories of the Institute of Applied Behavioral Science has recognized this need for encouraging volunteers and developing their skills by developing a Center for a Voluntary Society.

Riessman (1965) has surveyed the evidence in nonprofessional and peer-helper studies and has concluded that the benefits for the helper come from demands of the specific helping role, increased feelings of prestige, and awareness of new ways in which the helper is perceived and treated. Riessman suggests also that placing persons who request help, such as drug users wanting to quit, in small helper roles starts a spiraling growth process whereby the helpers' motivations for self-improvement and learning of helping skills gradually increase. Then they are added to the pool of people with high level helping skills to be shared with others. Thus, the "multiplier effect" is put in motion.

You probably recognize a paradox here. Whereas the helping process exists ostensibly for the development of the helpee, we need to recognize the reality of the helper's needs for growth and satisfaction through the helping relationship also.

Helping Is Learning Self-Help

Helping is also a process of encouraging the helpee to learn how to learn. In the helping process helpees learn more effective ways of coping with their present feelings and environmental demands, as well as techniques for solving personal problems, methods of planning, and techniques for discriminating among value choices. Thus, by learning a process of self-help, helpees not only satisfy their present needs, but also learn how to meet future needs as well. One of the most helpful services we can perform for others is to create conditions where they can learn how to solve problems with their own resources. People can be taught, for example, to make decisions and solve problems without the aid of a helper by following the steps under positive action in Figure 2.

FIGURE 2. HELPING SKILLS

For Understanding

1. Listening
   - 1.1 Attending
   - 1.2 Paraphrasing
   - 1.3 Clarifying
   - 1.4 Perception checking
2. Leading
   - 2.1 Indirect leading
   - 2.2 Direct leading
   - 2.3 Focusing
   - 2.4 Questioning
3. Reflecting
   - 3.1 Feeling
   - 3.2 Content
   - 3.3 Experience
4. Summarizing
   - 4.1 Feeling
   - 4.2 Content
   - 4.3 Process
5. Confronting
   - 5.1 Describing feelings
   - 5.2 Expressing feelings
   - 5.3 Feeding back
   - 5.4 Meditating
   - 5.5 Repeating
   - 5.6 Associating
6. Interpreting
   - 6.1 Explaining
   - 6.2 Questioning
   - 6.3 Fantasizing
7. Informing
   - 7.1 Giving information
   - 7.2 Giving advice
   - 7.3 Suggesting

For Comfort and Crisis Utilization

1. Supporting
   - 1.1 Contacting
   - 1.2 Reassuring
   - 1.3 Relaxing
2. Crisis intervening
   - 2.1 Building hope
   - 2.2 Consoling
   - 2.3 Controlling
   - 2.4 Developing alternatives
3. Centering
   - 3.1 Identifying strengths
   - 3.2 Reviewing growth experiences
   - 3.3 Recalling peak experiences
4. Referring

For Positive Action

1. Problem solving and decision making
   - 1.1 Identifying problems
   - 1.2 Changing problems to goals
   - 1.3 Analyzing problems
   - 1.4 Exploring alternatives and implications
   - 1.5 Planning a course of action
   - 1.6 Generalizing to new problems
2. Behavior changing
   - 2.1 Modeling
   - 2.2 Rewarding
   - 2.3 Extinguishing
   - 2.4 Desensitizing

Helping Skills for Understanding, Comfort, and Action

A Two-Stage Helping Model

Helping skills are used in various combinations to meet two major purposes—establishing a relationship and facilitating action. Many of the skills listed in Figure 2 under *understanding* and *comfort* are used early in the helping process to find out what the person wants and to create a climate for helping. Then, when a relationship of trust is established and the choice alternatives are more clear, more of the *action* methods come into prominence. Details of this process model are described in chapter 3.

Classification of Skills

There is no standard classification of helping skills or common vocabulary. Goodman and Dooley (1976) surveyed a number of classification schemes for what they called "help-intended communications." These helping intentions were carried out in six "response modes," gleaned from several helping systems, as follows: (1) questioning, (2) advisement, (3) silence, (4) interpretation, (5) reflection, and (6) self-disclosure. The main question is, what categories are most meaningful in training helpers? All helping styles include skills that facilitate expression, awareness, or understanding of feelings, and those that facilitate rational problem solving, decision making, and acting. Figure 2 contains a classification of these skills, which include those found by Goodman and Dooley to be most meaningful and simple. The three categories of understanding, comfort, and action reflect the main helping process goals that are translations of what helpees usually want. These three functional categories are overlapping in the sense that methods for promoting understanding also provide comfort and facilitate action.

The following chapters will present the basic helping skills to include outcome behaviors expected in the helpee. Although there is little research on the relationship between helper behavior and consequent helpee behavior, there is a body of experience and a set of hypotheses about the connections from which to draw. Steps in the format for the three chapters on skills are: (1) what the skill is; (2) purposes for using it; (3) illustrations of its use; (4) outcomes expected for the helpee; (5) summary of guidelines for using the skill.

Expected Outcomes

After reading this chapter you can: (1) describe your own needs to be helpful; (2) identify three sources of personal gain to the helper from engaging in the helping process; (3) identify the basic purpose and point of view of this book; (4) identify the nature of help in terms of fulfilling needs and encouraging responsible independence; (5) identify three arguments supporting and three refuting the value of professional and nonprofessional approaches to helping; (6) describe and cite examples of self-help, peer, cross-age, and community helper projects; and (7) list twelve basic skill clusters in the areas of understanding, comfort, and action. We will look now at the personal characteristics of an effective helper.

Suggestions for Further Study

Caplan, G., and Killilea, M., *Support Systems and Mutual Systems.* New York: Grune & Stratton, 1976. (A collection of articles on mutual support and self-help programs.)

Carkhuff, R., *Helping and Human Relations.* New York: Holt, Rinehart & Winston, 1969. (A two-volume description of a model for developing helping skills.)

Combs, A., Avila, D., and Purkey, W., *Helping Relationships: Basic Concepts for the Helping Professions.* Boston: Allyn & Bacon, 1971. (An overview of the helping relationship from a phenomenological viewpoint.)

———, *The Helping Relationship Sourcebook.* Boston: Allyn & Bacon, 1972. (A collection of readings from many authors on the helping process, mainly from a phenomenological view.)

Danish, S. J., and Hauer, A. L., *Helping Skills: A Basic Training Program.* New York: Behavioral Publications, 1973. (Ch. 1 includes a laboratory approach to understanding one's needs to be a helper.)

Fenlason, A., Ferguson, G., and Abrahamson, A., *Essentials in Interviewing.* 2nd ed. New York: Harper & Row, 1962. (A general overview of the interviewing process, methods, and essential attitudes.)

Rogers, C., "Characteristics of a helping relationship." *Personnel and Guidance Journal* 37 (1958); 6–16. (An early descriptive effort to define some dimensions of helping by a behavioral scientist.)

TWO

Characteristics of Helpers

Why Is Helping Effective in Assisting People to Grow?

A growing body of evidence indicates that the personal qualities of helpers are as significant for positive growth of helpees as are the methods they use. Effective and ineffective helpers cannot be distinguished, therefore, by their techniques, but they definitely can be contrasted on their personal beliefs and traits (Combs et al. 1969).

In this chapter I will focus on helper attitudinal characteristics and their implications, and in the following chapters I will cover methods for communicating these helping attitudes to helpees. Outcomes you can expect from studying this chapter are that you will be able to: (1) cite the key findings of three researchers on helper characteristics; (2) list and illustrate six general characteristics of helpers and five facilitative conditions determined by helper personal traits; (3) describe five levels of functioning; (4) describe the relationship between helper interview style and helper life style; and (5) list motives for wanting to be a helper.

This chapter includes extensive lists and overviews of research on helper characteristics. To facilitate application of this material to your helping practices, keep a log of these traits and rate yourself. Thus you'll be able to judge yourself and receive feedback from friends on whether you possess the trait listed, whether it functions effectively for you, or whether it needs improvement.

Combs and his coworkers studied some basic beliefs about people and self-help by contrasting various helpers from counseling, teaching, and the ministry with nonhelpers. The helpers perceived other people as *able* rather than unable to solve their own problems and manage their lives. People were perceived also as *dependable, friendly,* and *worthy.* Helpers had self-perceptions and traits distinct from non-helpers, such as identification with *people* rather than things, adequate *capacity to cope* with problems rather than lack of problem solving ability, and more *self-revelation* and willingness to be themselves than self-concealing.

Rogers (1961) concluded from his experience and reviews of research that the helper's theory and method were far less important for an effective helping relationship than manifestations of the helper's *attitudes.* Rogers noted also that it was the helpee's *perception* of the helper's attitudes that made a difference in effectiveness. Research has confirmed what the life experience of most of us has indicated, namely, that the helpful person needs to be an attractive, friendly person, someone with whom you feel comfortable, and someone whose opinions you value. The helpful person inspires confidence and trust.

Levels and Styles of Functioning

An important consideration is the helper's level of functioning in a helping relationship. Carkhuff and Berenson (1967), describe five levels of functioning for six interview dimensions. Level 3 on the empathy dimension, for example, refers to the minimum level of feeling response necessary to be effective. Empathy is that essential quality of putting one's self in the place of the other, even to the point of experiencing feelings as the other does. Level 2 means empathizing very little and at a level that detracts from helpee functioning. Level 1 means that no empathy is taking place. Levels 4 and 5, according to Carkhuff and Berenson, mean high levels of helper empathy are evident. The same high level of functioning should be noted in the helper's ability to express his or her ideas accurately, to identify feelings correctly, and to communicate clearly. Respect or regard, genuineness, concreteness, and warmth can be scaled similarly from the highest of level 5 to the lowest, level 1.

Carkhuff and his associates (1969) have presented convincing evidence that if the helper is functioning at a high level in regard to *impor-*

tant facilitative conditions, constructive changes will take place in the helpee. The converse is true also: A low level of helper functioning can have destructive consequences for the helpee. Similarly, if the helper is functioning at the same level as the helpee no change is likely to take place.

All helper characteristics can be scaled. As a practical application of this concept on levels of functioning I suggest you develop a simple rating scale, similar to the scale shown in this chapter, for the helper characteristics described below. As you learn to facilitate the growth of others, rate yourself on this scale. Ask your peers who observe your helping efforts to rate you also.

Facilitative Characteristic Levels

Level 5

Present consistently in helping exchanges

Quality of helper response consistently high

Level 4

Present most of the time in helping exchanges

Quality of helper response high 75 percent of the time

Level 3

Minimum and sporadic presence of helping characteristic—at least half the time

Quality of helping characteristic barely facilitative—minimal effectiveness

Level 2

Some evidence of helping characteristic present—at least 10 percent of the time

Quality of helping response extremely low

Level 1

No evidence of this helper characteristic in helping exchanges

It would be simple if we could relate facilitative characteristics to specific methods that the helper uses, but this condition is impossible at this stage of knowledge, especially considering the wide variations in style among individual helpers. The following facilitative characteristics, which have been identified in a wide range of studies, embody elements of many divergent helping styles and theories. As a result, they have wide application to many helping relationships. Rogers, for example, stresses the essential contribution of helper personal traits to the broad helping process. Others, who emphasize behavior change, stress methods of changing the environment rather than helper attitudes, although the current trend is to emphasize both attitudes and the technology of behavior change.

Helping and Helper Life Style

Another facet of the facilitative conditions described below is their natural outgrowth of helper life style. These conditions are not stylized traits that helpers turn on and off, but are characteristic of their lives outside of the helping relationship. If they are not living these conditions they tend to be perceived by helpees as artificial and incongruous. The helper's life must thus be planned in a satisfying manner and lived according to the ideals of the effective and self-actualized person. In addition to enriching the everyday events of living, the helper must pay attention to continuous renewal and revitalization, periodically examining his or her life goals, clarifying personal values, setting new directions, and discovering new sources of energy. To avoid obsolescence, professional helpers must keep up with the rapid changes in the concepts and methods of helping. All helpers, however, need renewal experiences to counter the draining effects of continuous demanding contact with people. Teachers, for example, are vulnerable to the "burnout" effect, unless they plan systematically for renewal experiences to regain their enthusiasm, energy, and effectiveness. Some of the indicators of such needed renewal are increasing irritability, low energy level, cynicism about people, indifference to the suffering of others, loss of self-confidence, and general malaise. While the helping process has some built-in renewal potential, most helpers find that they must seek their renewal outside of their helping relationships.

Matching Helpers and Helpees

Although much research has been done on helper characteristics, helpee traits, and helping methods, very little has been done on the interaction of helper and helpee. Growing evidence from research supports our common sense observations that the compatibility of helper and helpee personalities is a key factor in a successful relationship.

If we could match helpers and helpees on basic styles in advance, we might produce more successful outcomes. For example, type A and type B helpers have been identified as having differential effects on helpees (Whitehorn and Betz 1960, Carson 1967). Type A is more "approaching" and interested in feelings, whereas type B is less approaching and more cognitively oriented. Helping relationships of A types were characterized by greater trust, and helpees were approached in a more active personal way than was typical of B types. In the near future it may be possible to develop training experiences that will match particular methods and helper styles with specific needs of helpees so that maximum outcomes can be achieved.

The Helper Personality

No cluster of traits describes a people-helper who is universally effective. Research on counselor and teacher effectiveness indicates that although there is no fixed trait pattern for effective helping, there are strong indications of desirable conditions that facilitate constructive helpee changes (Carkhuff 1969, Combs 1969, Rogers 1961). I include the essence of these findings and their implications to serve as a tentative template of traits and behaviors that you can place on yourself. You must realize, however, that this list of characteristics is a composite from research and opinions of experienced helpers rather than a model of essential qualities and conditions for all helpers. I will present first some general helper characteristics, to be followed by a list of more specific facilitative traits and growth conditions created by the helper.

Helper Personal Characteristics

A general dictum among people helpers says that if I want to become more effective I must begin with myself; our personalities are thus the principal tools of the helping process. Combs (1969) used the term "self as instrument" to indicate that our principal helping tool is ourselves acting spontaneously in response to the rapidly changing interpersonal demands of the helping relationship. A teacher must react to new stimuli instantly, for example, with little or no thought ahead of time. How the teacher reacts is a function of who he or she is at that moment and how the relationship with that particular student is seen. We are behavior models for helpees no matter how we construe our helping role. They imitate our behaviors, identify with our views, and absorb our values. Although we may try to be impartial and objective helpers, the facts indicate that we cannot be such and still remain involved in the relationship. The following helper characteristics determine the nature of this relationship.

1. Awareness of Self and Values. There is universal agreement among practitioners and writers that helpers need a broad awareness of their own value positions. They must be able to answer very clearly the questions, Who am I? and What is important to me? This awareness aids helpers in being honest with themselves and their helpees, and assists them also in avoiding unwarranted or unethical use of helpees for the helpers' own need satisfactions. As I indicated in chapter 1, the relationship is a process of mutual need fulfillment, but helpers must know the limits of using the helping relationship for fulfilling their own psychological needs. Self-awareness provides some insurance, furthermore, against the tendency to project values onto others. In every human relationship a fantasy of the other person makes up a large part of our image of that person. For example, I may perceive the helpee from a few minimal cues as a very undependable person. The question is always, How much of this judgment is really descriptive of that person and how much is myself projected? Am I putting on others my own views of what is dependable? Dependability is a judgment; it is not a very descriptive term for behavior. Am I judging the person against some vague social norm?

While we may have opinions about traits of people we like and want to associate with, one characteristic of effective helpers is that they try to suspend judgments of others. Although it may be helpful sometimes to confront helpees with our opinions, we should try to describe specific behaviors and to avoid labels, mainly because so frequently they are projections of our own social values.

Numerous helping situations test the helper's values. If a helpee is describing a sexual behavior that the helper finds unacceptable, or if the helpee is talking about divorce and the helper has strong convictions about the inviolability of marriage contracts, how does the helper behave? Can helpers maintain their own values and still accept the helpees? Can they empathize, yet be keenly aware of their own values as helpers and their tendencies to project those values?

How do helpers acquire this kind of awareness? Obtaining counseling for themselves or participating in awareness groups are key sources of self-awareness. Reflection and meditation are other means. Self-renewal workshops focusing on examination of values and getting in touch with one's self are becoming sources of expanded awareness and renewed vigor to continue in demanding helping relationships.

2. *Ability to Analyze the Helper's Own Feelings.* Observations of helping specialists suggest that one needs to be "cool," to be detached from one's feelings. While effective helping implies awareness and control of one's feelings to prevent the projection of needs described above, we must realize that helpers also are *feeling* all the time. They feel, for example, the elation of helpee growth toward independence. Similarly, they feel disappointed when their own expectations for helpee growth do not develop. They feel depreciated when their overtures of help are

spurned by helpees. Knowing the reasons why helpee esteem needs require this kind of "rejecting" behavior is of some comfort, but helpers are inclined to respond with feelings of disappointment to others who do not value their efforts.

It is necessary to promote a feeling of confidence in the helper; and there seems to be a nice balance between the stance of the know-it-all expert and the self-effacing attitude that says, "I don't have any special talent or skill; I'm just little old me!" Am I aware, for example, of my tendencies to depreciate myself as a helper on the one hand, or my tendency to act like a "guru," one who has all the answers, on the other? Furthermore, why do I need to create a mystique about myself that promotes awe and dependency in the helpee? One of the interesting phenomena of human interaction is the charismatic effect. Some people appear to have intense auras of energy that affect others around them. Some of this effect is probably a placebo effect, meaning that through the power of suggestion, the helper's efforts or authoritative position bring results, no matter what he or she does. Weissberg (1977), after searching for an answer to the question, Why does counseling work? concluded that it was a "nagging" effect; by this he meant the active and challenging interventions performed by helpers that mobilize helpees into constructive action to solve their problems. Activities such as authoritative suggestions, assigned homework, and relentless urging are illustrations.

Helpers must learn to deal effectively with their confusion and value conflicts. When are self-assertion and expression of freedom important, for example, and when are conforming and adjusting the appropriate behaviors? The helper often is caught between liberating forces of growing independence and society's need to punish deviates, force conformity, and banish rebels. Helpers must learn to live with this basic human conflict in themselves and their helpees.

Feelings of power over helpees come quite unexpectedly. Unless helpers are wary, they can be trapped into smug controlling feelings when helpees express strong dependence on them, or when they indicate their helper has influence over them. When helpees express profuse gratitude, for example, I begin to wonder if I really provided a condition in which they felt they helped themselves, or whether they felt I did it for them. The latter feeling denies their own assertive self-help.

In addition to the personal power the helper may feel, it is important to be aware of the hidden dimensions of power in institutions. Governmental agencies, in particular, have certain regulatory responsibilities or legal mandates to offer services under specified conditions. Helpers in such agencies must be wary of identifying too closely with the power of the agency under the guise of carrying out the agency's mission. Often the helpee becomes lost in such settings, and the helping services tend to support the power of the organization. The result may be an exaggerated emphasis on adjustment or pacification rather than on actualization and liberation. An example in a school setting is the possibility of a helping staff member taking the management side and supporting the school's power over the students rather than focusing primarily on what is in the best growth interest of the students. It would be useful at this point to focus on the suggested activity in chapter 1 regarding assessment of your motives for helping. After your self-analysis and this discussion on power and dependency, to what extent do you find satisfaction in power over others, in seeing them dependent on and grateful to you, and in identifying with the power of your agency over its clientele?

Professional helpers label these unconscious feelings toward helpees as "countertransference effects," meaning that the helper's needs are expressed in behaviors such as dominating, overprotecting, loving, pleasing, seducing, or manipulating helpees. These feelings are "transferred" from the helper's own past relationships with significant people to the present relationship.

The only known antidotes to the kinds of behavior described above are awareness of one's particular tendencies to "transfer" one's own needs, problems, and unrecognized feelings to the helpee. This awareness can be obtained primarily through feedback about one's behavior in individual and group counseling experiences. Furthermore, one needs to have one's personal life in such good order that one can take disappointment, frustration, demanding confrontations, and intensive encounters in helping relationships without projecting them onto helpees, or developing personal symptoms such as depression, withdrawal, or physical complaints. As a helper one needs a strong ego, meaning confidence in one's own worth as a person. Again, as stated earlier under helper lifestyle, possible protections against self-defeating conditions can be found in a counseling relationship for one's self occasionally, and in a satisfying personal life to provide continuous self-renewal. Helping is an emotionally demanding activity, even when done informally, and some provisions must be made for helpers to "recharge their own batteries" occasionally.

3. *Ability to Serve as Model and Influencer.* Helpers function as models and social influences to their helpees, whether they want to or not. Much research literature shows the power of models for acquiring socially adaptive as well as maladaptive behaviors (Sarason and Ganzer 1971). It is more controversial, however, whether helpers must be

models also of decorum, maturity, and effectiveness in their personal lives. I have two reactions on this issue. The first is that helpers must have fulfilling lives, or they will tend to use the helping relationship too much for satisfaction of their own unmet needs. My second reaction is that helper credibility may be questioned if he or she has a chaotic personal life. If their marital lives are stormy, for example, or if their children have constant brushes with police, the validity of their work is likely to be questioned.

Helpers often are caught in the squeeze between their own self-fulfilling desires to deviate from local community norms and to resist pressures to conform, particularly if they are employed by local agencies such as schools and churches. Our society is reaching a point, however, where wide variations in behavior are acceptable, and where the private life of the prospective helper is respected. The final standard for judging the appropriateness of the helper's behavior is the helpee's judgment about the helper's usefulness in their present relationship.

Behaving like an "expert" helper in the eyes of the helpee is important to the helping relationship. Schmidt and Strong (1970) studied the behaviors seen as "expert" and "inexpert" from the helpee's viewpoint. Those helpers perceived as expert treated the student helpees as equals, with friendly attentive behavior. They spoke with confidence and liveliness. The "expert" helpers came prepared with knowledge about their helpees, their backgrounds and reasons for coming, and they moved quickly to the heart of the problem. Those perceived as "inexpert" were tense, fearful, rambling, uncertain, or overly cool and casual, communicating disinterest and boredom. Because of their more enthusiastic responsiveness to the helpees, the less experienced and less professionally trained counselors often were perceived as the "experts" by the student observers. To have influence with helpees, then, helpers must consider how they are perceived by their helpees and what kinds of models they are presenting.

The evidence about power and influence leaves no doubt that formal helping, in particular, is a strong influence process. Ivey (1977) and Egan (1975) see social influence theory as basic to the helping process. In a provocative article on therapy as manipulation Gillis (1974) makes a strong case for the success of formal helping being due largely to the influence and assertiveness of the helper.

4. Altruism. As described early in chapter 1, a vital question for the helper is, Why do I want to help? I stated earlier that helpers have needs too and that they expect some satisfactions to maintain their helping behaviors. It is not too productive to engage in extensive selfprobings about why one wants to help, but it is necessary to have some awareness that one is acting for one's self as well as for some assumed value for the helpee. It is evident, however, that the effective helper is very interested in people. In his studies of effective helpers, Combs (1969) found that a central value was their concern with people rather than things and with an altruistic stance moving outward toward helping people rather than a more narcissistic focus on themselves. The effective helpers also identified with humanity rather than seeing themselves separated from people.

When helpers are asked, Why do you help? they are likely to come up with pious statements designed to impress others with their expansive humanity and virtue. Honest feedback from colleagues, friends, and helpees is the key source of awareness of motives for helping. An example of helpful feedback would be statements such as, "I observe that you are spending much time with John, and that you talk much about him. I wonder to what extent your own concerns are intertwined with his. Could it be that your interest in helping him is to get some help for yourself, too?" Another source of awareness of one's motives is just to accept the probable fact that we have many basic needs and personal growth goals fulfilled by helping others. Such needs are self-worth, status, and intimacy. The standard for judging is the pleasure or pain experienced during and after a helping relationship; for example, "I just feel good about myself when I see people like Jane grow in social effectiveness." Just as some persons experience pleasure after creating a poem or playing a musical composition, so helpers experience a glow of satisfaction in witnessing human growth and realizing that they had some part in facilitating that growth.

Granted, we could rationalize altruism quickly in terms of need theory or reward-punishment principles, but the love motive, in the Greek "agape" sense of non-erotic personal caring, is strong in helpers. They believe they are helping out of a deep love of humanity focused on a particular person. This motive has strong theological overtones and reflects the helpers' profound commitment to a special view of the world and their place in it. Although I subscribe to a considerable portion of this kind of motivation for helping, I want to be sure my awareness "antennae" are tuned to feedback from the helpee so that I can check the validity of my views and the soundness of my motives. I want to know, for example, when my needs to convert others to my way of thinking and valuing, or to behave according to my model, become too strong.

It is my opinion that the Hebraic-Christian tradition has contributed in a solid way to the helping climate of our civilization through its ethic of unconditional service to others and its emphasis on the love motive.

Yet, like knives, drugs, or machines, helping motives quickly can become destructive tools in the hands of naive or zealous users.

Findings from studies on altruistic behavior have some relevance here (Baron and Liebert 1971). Seeing a *model* of helping, that is, watching someone in the act of helping someone else, tends to elicit similar behavior in the watchers. A strong *reciprocity* principle operates in altruistic behavior also. People tend to help those from whom they have received help, since American society has a strong "give and get" norm and a subtle system of social debts and credits. There is also a social *responsibility* factor operating, since people tend to help those who are dependent on them, even when the rewards for helping seem to be remote.

Interpersonal *attraction* was a principle operating in some of the helping studies. *Liking* the person and being of *similar background* promoted altruism. A compliance principle seemed to explain some behavior where helping was expected in order to obtain *social approval.* This brief discussion indicates that altruistic motives are extremely complex; it is likely that a variety of socially conditioned as well as consciously chosen values motivate helping acts.

General helping acts often grow out of strong social support and change motives. From the standpoint of our collective self-interest, and perhaps survival as a race, it is essential that people support one another. When they do not, all are jeopardized in the form of crime, accidents, and pollution. We must have more people concerned about the welfare of others if our society is to survive. And we need activist-helpers who are concerned primarily with changing social conditions to meet human welfare needs, rather than merely helping individuals to cope with the demands of an ailing society. A growing number of help-oriented people are working to change large systems rather than encouraging people to adjust to the system. Their goal is to create a people-serving and growth-facilitating society rather than to perpetuate destructive practices of present society.

5. Strong Sense of Ethics. When outlined clearly, personal beliefs about people and society serve as conscious guidelines for action. When one values the helpee's welfare, for example, one will do nothing to harm him or her. If someone asks for personal information confided to the helper, it will not be divulged. The helper would regard that information as a symbol of trust.

When these ethical principles are shared widely among helpers, they are written down and codified. Professional groups have such ethics codes, which serve as formal guidelines for action, and which reflect common values regarding helper-helpee relationships and responsibilities. The key value of a code to a helper is to provide some frame of reference for judgments about client welfare and social responsibility. For example, while their ultimate allegiance generally is to the society they serve, the primary responsibility of helpers is to their helpee clients. Information must not be revealed unless there is clear and imminent danger to the helpee or other people. The complexities and variations in circumstances make this topic too large for further discussion here, but you are encouraged to delve into the details of ethical principles and codes among the suggested readings. The main point to emphasize here is that helpers become committed to a set of ethical behaviors that are reflections of their own moral standards, society's codes, and the norms of the helping professions.

6. Responsibility. Related to helpers' ethical behavior is the issue of how much responsibility they can assume for their own and their helpees' behavior. Responsibility is a judgmental term defined only in terms of a specific helping context, but there are common understandings about responsible helper behavior. Helpers behave ethically, as defined above, meaning that they balance helpee welfare and social expectations. They know and respect their personal limitations, so that they do not promise unrealistic outcomes. They refer helpees to specialists when their limitations and their needs so dictate, and maintain contact until the specialist takes responsibility for a new relationship.

Helpers define their relationships to helpees in a manner clear to the helpees. The clear norm of professional helpers should, in my opinion, apply to all types of helpers; this norm says that, once a helping relationship is agreed on, the helper will do all in her or his power to make it productive until such time as a transfer of responsibility is made to another helper, or until either person voluntarily and formally terminates the relationship. In their first contact, the helper says, for example, "I see my task as helping to clarify the ways you see this problem and to look at some alternatives. You must then make the commitment to action and do something about it. If we can't work this out together, then we can explore possibilities of other people with whom you might work more effectively."

The issue of how much responsibility a helper can or should take for a helpee's behavior is very unclear. Some helpers move to one extreme of saying that the helpee is the only one responsible for the outcomes or consequences of the relationship. Others maintain a very accountable stance under the assumption that the helper is mainly responsible for what happens to the helpee as a result of the helping relationship. It is my observation that most authorities view this issue as a shared responsibility. They keep this question open and move along the responsibility continuum according to their best judgment of the specific condition and age of the helpee. Helpees are responsible for their own decisions, for example, including how much of themselves they are ready to reveal. The helper is responsible for presenting ideas, reactions, or support as deemed appropriate or as requested by the helpee.

There is a misperception about responsible behavior in regard to helpees revealing personal data about themselves. It is commonly assumed that no harm is done if the helper just listens to the helpee; but listening has a powerful uncovering effect on the helpee. Helpees often pull down their protective psychological armor while they become more open. The effect on the helpee is often a feeling of vulnerability and hurt or, sometimes, fear over having revealed too much. One of the ways helpees tell us this is by not showing up for another session. Responsible helper behavior is knowing when to forestall these self-revelations or expressions of feeling. One of the great dilemmas of helping is that we can't be helpful if helpees are not open, yet the most helpful thing we might do is to discourage them from revealing too much about themselves.

Helper as Scholar-Researcher

Thoughtful helpers soon realize that they must have some framework for ordering their experiences with helpees. When they begin to question their assumptions about people, the effectiveness of their helping approach, or the validity of helping in general, they are *thinking* like behavioral scientists. When they systematically collect data about helping behavior, make valid inferences, generalize carefully, and form conclusions about those data, they are *acting* like behavioral scientists.

The critical helper sees the need for more information about the process, more effective skills, and more useful theories about people and the helping function. So the helper turns scholar by reading about others' experience in helping and the results of specialized research reports.

Although not all helpers can or should become behavioral science researchers, they need to have the critical thinking and observational skills of the scientist. The actual research techniques for validating procedures and discovering new knowledge are part of professional helpers' education, but even they tend to leave the bulk of formal research to specialists. All people helpers are scholars, though, when they read and apply results from books and journals.

While research evidence (Joslin 1965) and experience indicate that one can be an effective helper without extensive formal education, the helping function draws on the ideas of, and raises many questions related to, the disciplines of philosophy, biology, psychology, sociology, and anthropology, as well as literature and the arts. In other words, the helper's possibilities for flexibility and effectiveness increase as his or her own cultural awareness expands. Helpers must be committed, in any case, to the ideal of lifelong learning to avoid obsolescence and to maximize their helping effectiveness. This commitment is expressed in the form of following a reading program, accepting feedback on skills, and working toward personal development.

As helpers become more involved, they develop increasing interest in the social context of helping. They find, for example, that the helpee's background as a social minority member, an immigrant, or a resident of a particular urban subculture has a profound effect on the helpee's outlook and life style. Understanding the helpee's background provides a sounder basis for empathy, understanding, and later interventions in the helping relationship.

Helper as Growth Facilitator

Since the principal helping function stressed in this book is facilitating achievement of helpee growth goals, some supporting data for growth facilitator characteristics are needed. This role of helper as *growth facilitator* is different from more traditional models of helping, such as the priest model, the medical model, and the behavioral engineer model. Of these alternate approaches, the *priest model* focuses on conducting ceremonials, interpreting sacred writings, and providing spiritual support. This help consists of supporting, prescribing rules for living, and providing outside intervention. The helper's goals are to make one's lot in this life more effective, and to prepare for the next. Another traditional model we all know well is the *medical approach,* where diagnosis of complaints and application of treatments are the key features. The helpful elements include being told what is wrong and being given treatment, surgery, or prescriptions for correcting the disease condition. The *behavioral engineer model* stresses management of the environment. This help approach consists of changing the physical and psychological environment to meet essential human needs. Although these descriptions are oversimplifications of other helping models, they are cited as contrasts to our *growth facilitator model* of helping.

Rogers (1957) specified six essential interview conditions for helpee development. Among them are *congruence* (meaning consistency and genuineness) in the relationship, *unconditional positive regard* for the helpee, *empathic understanding* of the helpee's internal frame of reference, and *efforts to communicate* this understanding. Although there has been controversy over whether Rogers' conditions are essential and sufficient, there is wide agreement that the helper conditions he cites are very desirable. Most helpers agree, for example, that positive regard is important, but few assert that this regard must always be *unconditional* to be helpful. Several investigators over the past few years have checked the relationship between these and other facilitative traits with helpee behavior outcomes. Some of the more productive studies are those of Truax and Carkhuff (1967), Combs et al. (1969), and Carkhuff (1969). Results of these and similar studies are described in the remainder of this chapter.

1. Helper Empathy. Empathy is the principal route to understanding helpees and enabling them to feel understood. The helper sees the world the way helpees perceive it, that is, from their "internal frame of reference." Helpers make an active effort to put themselves in this internal perceptual frame without losing their own identity or objectivity. They do this largely by thinking *with* rather than *for* or *about* the helpees, as indicated in Figure 3. The word *empathy* derives from the German word *Einfühlung* meaning "feeling into." It is related to the kind of response that sports spectators give when they lean forward with the jumper. Similarly, helpers tend to "feel into" helpees' feeling experiences as they talk.

The helper tries to become an alternate self for the helpee, a kind of

FIGURE 3. INTERNAL AND EXTERNAL FRAMES OF REFERENCE

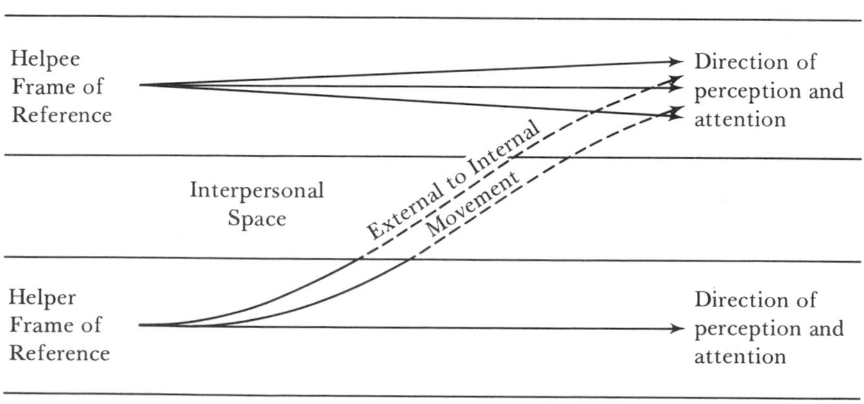

emotional mirror. The main criterion of success for helper empathy is whether helpees can use the helpers' empathic understanding for their own self-understanding and consequent confidence in their ability to solve their own problems. To function at a minimum level, the helper must respond accurately to covert feelings as well as to the overt content. Briefly, then, helpers manifest empathy through this ability to perceive what is going on in the helpee's feelings and to communicate this perception clearly to the helpee. Figure 3 illustrates these internal and external frames of reference. Helpers and helpees are moving from left to right in their own ways of perceiving the world. The helper, for example, thinks how he or she can move from the lower left corner across the personal space that separates them, such that the helper can begin to perceive the world the way the helpee sees it (the internal frame of reference). At the same time helpers are adding something of themselves and their worlds to this process.

Helpers enter the internal frame of reference by listening attentively and asking themselves several questions: *What* is the helpee *feeling* right now? *How* does he view this *problem*? *What* does she see in her *world*? The helper who is thinking from an external or diagnostic frame of reference is asking "why" questions as, *Why* is the helpee so upset? What is *causing* the problem? Judgments are made, such as, He's *upset* and seems to be in bad shape; I've got to help him. The external frame, then, is the helper's attempt to understand the helpee from an observer stance using an intellectual problem-solving framework. Combs (1969) found his effective helpers used an internal rather than external framework for perceiving their helpees. The external may be an appropriate approach for some stages in the helping process but not when the goal is to understand helpee feelings.

Since so much helping is done over the telephone in crisis centers and informal counseling situations, the question of face-to-face contact for empathy is significant. A study by Dilley, Lee, and Verrill (1971) in which face-to-face, confessional type, and phone contacts were used found no differences in helpers' ability to communicate empathy in the three methods. This study suggests that more helping could take place effectively over telephones.

In Figure 3 the helper tries to think and feel like the helpee. The helpee must be sufficiently open to allow the helper to direct a high proportion of attention and emotional energy toward the goal of working within the helpee's framework. This condition is difficult to achieve, particularly in helping situations in which the participants are far apart in race, age, experience, or socioeconomic status (Brammer and Shostrom 1977). Operationally, empathy is demonstrated when the helper indicates that the helpee's message is heard accurately with no additions or deletions.

The converse condition of too much empathy on the helper's part could be a problem too, perpetuating a dependent immaturity. As illustrated in Figure 3, helpers maintain a sense of independent direction in their own perceptual tracks as they attempt to get within their helpees' framework. If they move too fast and too completely into their helpees' frame, they are likely to lose their objectivity and sense of direction. Through this overidentification with the helpee, the helper is likely to be perceived as more sympathetic than empathic. Even when he or she maintains a strong empathic stance, there is the ever-present likelihood that the helpee's problem becomes the helper's burden too!

2. *Helper Warmth and Caring.* These related terms refer to key emotional response qualities in the helper, and they often accompany empathic efforts. Warmth is a condition of friendliness and considerateness manifested by smiling, eye contact, and nonverbal attending behaviors. Showing concern and interest such as offering a chair, looking after the person's comfort, and making the person feel valued are also means by which to show warmth.

Caring is a term closely related to warmth, but it is regarded as more enduring and intense emotionally; it means showing deep and genuine concern about the welfare of the helpee. The act of caring has strong affectional overtones also, meaning that it is a way of saying "I like you."

Some helpers speak of warmth and caring as mild types of nonpossessive love for the helpee which meet needs for response and affection. Early in this century Freud and his followers emphasized warmth as a significant factor in therapeutic power. Warmth in the helper conveys a personal psychological closeness, as opposed to professional distance. (Lack of therapist warmth can have unwanted effects. Hadley and Strupp (1976) found that such helper qualities as coldness, need to analyze, excessive emphasis on helpee transformation, and hostility contributed to these harmful effects.)

The helping skill involved here is how to convey this feeling of closeness, affection, and caring concern to the helpee without emotional entanglements, offensive forwardness, or threat of seduction. Some helpees, for example, have been so hurt by life that they cannot deal effectively with warmth when proffered, so alert helpers will adjust their behaviors to reduce the threat. Neither will they be embarrassed or upset when their helpees respond with cool detachment. In some social groups, emotional involvement with another makes one vulnerable to rejection and obligates one to the person offering the warmth.

A second helper concern is how much warmth to exhibit at different stages in the helping process. Although helpers do not turn warmth on and off, they are aware of the facilitative or debilitative effect of such emotional behavior on the helpee, and adjust accordingly. For example, showing warmth and caring are especially helpful in the early stages when the relationship is being built. They are helpful also when the helpee is going through a crisis, where the supportive value of helper warmth is especially desirable. Professional helpers for the past 60 years have written about the importance of warmth for a productive helping relationship. It is only recently, however, that research results have supported the facilitative effects of warmth and caring (Truax and Carkhuff 1964).

3. *Helper Openness.* One of the principal goals in the beginning of a helping relationship is to encourage helpees to disclose their thoughts and feelings freely to their helpers. This self-disclosure is related to their helpers' openness, since helpers must be willing to reveal their own views to their helpees in an honest way. Combs (1969) found that effective helpers were able to use self-revelation in building a constructive relationship. The essential condition of trust, furthermore, is directly dependent on the extent to which helper and helpee are open to one another.

Like so many helper characteristics, openness is paradoxical in that too much self-revelation on the part of the helper confuses the issue as to who is helpee and who is helper. Helpers need to be aware when their needs begin to supersede those of their helpees. The only general guideline that I can suggest is that helpers reveal only enough of themselves to facilitate the helpee's self-disclosure at the level of functioning desired. Helpers reveal themselves in a progressively free manner natural to a developing relationship. Too rapid disclosure on their part may overwhelm helpees with unexpected behavior or threaten them with too much personal data.

A term that Rogers (1961) and other writers use in this context is *genuineness*. This is a state where helpers' words are congruent or consistent with their actions. If a helper says, for example, "I'm glad to see you," he or she reflects this feeling with body language and voice quality consistent with the words of welcome.

Another word used in helping contexts is *authentic*—the opposite of fake; the helper tries not to hide behind a professional role or facade. A certain amount of social game-playing behavior may be appropriate early in the process when, for example, he or she says conventional things like, "Hello, how are you?" Effective helpers concentrate on listening and trying to understand what the helpee is feeling so that they can respond with appropriate and authentic feelings. The helper uses discretion in expressing negative feelings about the helpee at this stage, however, since such expressions may be destructive.

Carkhuff (1969) distinguishes between two stages of genuineness. The first involves a low level of functioning in recognition of the natural way trusting relationships develop. The helper is also in a *responsive* set, listening to the helpee. In the second stage of genuineness helpers are in an *initiative* set where they are more freely themselves as persons, thus enabling the helpees to be more expressive. Carkhuff emphasizes the modeling effect of the helper in this stage. The open quality of communication exhibited by the helper serves as an example for the helpee, and leads to a relationship where the helpee learns to be more open and genuine.

Congruence is another term used in helping professions to express the correspondence or harmony between the helper's behaviors, such as words, and his or her basic attitudes (Rogers 1951). Congruence refers also to helpers' credibility. They are perceived as more believable when their behavior and attitudes appear to "ring true" to the helpee. Perceiving helpers as congruent facilitates the helpees' congruence between their own words and feelings because of the modeling effect described above. When helpers, for example, say they are interested in the helpee's problem, their words should be consistent with their basic feelings; otherwise the discrepancy will be apparent to the helpees. The consequences very likely would be loss of confidence in the helper or annoyance at the helper's feigned interest.

4. *Helper Positive Regard and Respect.* This characteristic is an attitudinal set that expresses not only helpers' deep concerns for their helpees' welfare but also respect for their individuality and worth as persons. Rogers (1961) expresses this condition as "unconditional positive regard," meaning a nonjudgmental, "no-reservations" attitude. It says to helpees that they are free to be themselves and that they will be respected for it. The literature on helping shows that the term *unconditional* appears to be controversial. It means that no conditions or judgments will hamper the helpee's expression of feelings or ideas. I consider unconditionality relative to stages in the process of helping. In the first contacts it is important to convey through acceptance and warmth the attitude that "I neither approve nor disapprove of what you are saying. I want you to express yourself freely, and I will respect your right to feel as you please and to act as you feel within the limits of our mutual welfare. I want you to become your most real and effective self. Furthermore, I want to like you and respect you as a person."

Later in the helping process, when the relationship is well established, the helper begins to experience a variety of feelings toward the helpee. Then the regard becomes more conditional. Helpers express more of their own approving and disapproving attitudes, thus tending to reinforce or diminish certain behaviors in helpees. The helper's spontaneous and authentic behaviors become more apparent as the trust level deepens and the helpee is more open to honest feedback from the helper.

The principal vehicles for expressing regard and respect are words matched with genuine nonverbal expressions of warmth, acceptance, and empathy. Helpers convey an attitude that their help is being given with the condition that the helpees express honest feelings and attempt to become their best selves on their own terms. The helpee is not required to please or conform to the wishes of the helper. This respectful stance is facilitated by conscious efforts to be freeing rather than controlling or manipulating. Combs (1969) found such an approach was used effectively by the helpers in his study.

5. *Helper Concreteness and Specificity.* A key facilitating condition for accurate and clear communication in helping is the helper's attempt to be specific rather than general or vague. The effective helper models concreteness, but also confronts the helpee about specificity and clarity. When dealing with painful and unacceptable feelings, for example, there is a tendency to be abstract and circuitous to avoid direct confrontation with those feelings. Painful feelings tend to be stated in vague and elusive language in the beginning. In this instance the helper may say, for example, "You appear to be uneasy; most people seem to be uneasy in new situations." Another example is, "Please give me a specific example of what you feel right now." The strategy is to confront helpees with requests for *their* specific and present feelings stated in concrete terms. Using general phrases, such as "most people," "they say," or "it seems we," detract from the specific personal reference desired in the form of "I feel" or "I think that."

The helper assists the helpee to focus more on present, rather than past or future, concerns and feelings through questions and reflections. Helpers also model good examples of specific communication by using clear "I" statements. That is, he or she speaks in terms of "I think" or "I feel," rather than "People say" or "They think that."

One problem in using and encouraging specific expressions is that they may tend to reduce the spontaneity and free association of helpees' expressions of feeling. So often helpees wander about, tapping sensitive areas cautiously. This issue must be resolved according to the helper's best judgment. Typically, helpers might encourage and model specificity and concreteness of expression early in the process. Then, when their helpees become more involved, allow them more freedom to express themselves in their natural verbal style. Finally, when the process develops to the point of planning specific courses of action and when it demands a problem-solving approach, greater emphasis can then be placed on specificity and concreteness of expression and action.

Since helping is so dependent on clear communication, it follows that a key characteristic of the effective helper is *communication competence.* Research in linguistics and explorations in communication, such as that by Bandler and Grinder (1975) and Ivey (1977), underscore this quality as essential to effective helping. Bandler and Grinder, for example, indicate how helping clarifies helpee sentences, gives helpees better ways to describe themselves, and provides them with sharper descriptive thoughts about their problems. The discussion of the cultural basis for effective helping in chapter 1 is relevant here also, since helpers owe much of their effectiveness to being able to communicate within the language framework of their helpees.

A Concluding Statement

After reviewing the ideal helper's personal characteristics, one is struck with their paradoxical simplicity, yet complexity, for facilitating growth in helpees. Most of the conditions described in this chapter are extensions of ordinary effective human qualities. The relevant research and cumulative experience of professional helpers points out the necessity, however, for examining continuously the amount and timing of these growth-facilitating conditions for particular helpees at special moments in their development.

Also important is the need to be *flexible* as a people helper. At times one must be deeply personal, immersing one's self in the relationship, and at other times one must be an objective observer, studying the process carefully. Helpers must be able to move freely along the full range of these facilitating characteristics so that they can respond appropriately to helpee needs at different stages in the helping process. On the one hand this must be a natural intuitive process, and on the other hand it needs to be a deliberate rational process of sizing up and meeting helpee needs. Although this artistry comes naturally to some, it is most often an outcome of intensive and extensive effort and criticism.

However one construes the helping process—primarily as an art or as a science—it is essential that serious helpers take periodic looks at the assumptions they make about themselves, their helpees, and the helping process. This chapter focused on the helper as a person and how he or she uses this personhood as a helping tool. In the last chapter I will explore the idea of helpers as thinking beings who reflect on their work and develop a rationale for their help. Various models are presented for helper self-criticism and for describing what they are doing and why they are doing it.

Expected Outcomes

You can: (1) name three research investigators of helper characteristics and cite their key findings; (2) list six general behavioral characteristics of helpers; (3) cite and illustrate five growth-facilitating conditions for helping relationships through helper personal qualities and values; (4) describe five levels of functioning; (5) describe the close relationship between helper interview style and helper life style; and (6) list motives for wanting to be a helper. The final criterion of successful mastery of the ideas in this chapter is your demonstrated ability to live a whole and creative life in and out of your helping relationships.

Suggestions for Further Study

American Psychological Association, *Ethical Standards of Psychologists.* Washington, D.C.: American Psychological Association, 1953 (Proposal for modification: 1977).

Brammer, L., and Shostrom, E., *Therapeutic Psychology: Fundamentals of Actualization Counseling and Psychotherapy.* 3rd ed. Englewood Cliffs, N.J.: Prentice-Hall, 1977. (Ch. 6 on characteristics of the therapeutic psychologist.)

Egan, G., *The Skilled Helper.* Monterey, Ca.: Brooks/Cole, 1976. (Ch. 1 section on the portrait of a helper.)

Ethical Standards, American Personnel and Guidance Association, *Personnel and Guidance Journal* 40 (1961); 206–9.

Hamechek, D., *Encounters with the Self.* New York: Holt, Rinehart & Winston, 1971. (A comprehensive survey of principles and research findings on development and understanding of the self, especially ch. 7 on developing a healthy self-image.)

Rogers, C., *On Becoming a Person.* Boston: Houghton Mifflin, 1961. (A collection of Professor Rogers' papers on various personal aspects of the helping function.)

THREE

The Helping Process

This chapter is intended as a map through the complicated pathways of helping. It will list typical sequential events in the helping process and cite some of the problems encountered at each stage. The term *process* thus refers to the ongoing events and their meaning to the participants. Each stage in the process requires a special skills cluster. In the beginning, for example, understanding and support skills are prominent in building the working relationship; in the later stages, decision and action skills are more needed. Methods for handling problems in the process stages will be covered in chapters 4 through 6. All helpers must decide early in the process whether to focus on the person or to work directly to change environmental conditions. The process and methods described in this book assume that the helper decides to work directly with the person.

Outcomes You Can Expect

From reading this chapter you should be able to: (1) describe the dimensions and stages in a typical helping process; (2) list the functions of a helping relationship; (3) act more confidently when facing some of the problems encountered in the various stages; and (4) develop your own cognitive map of the helping process on which you can place your ideas and methods about help. The ultimate criterion of successful study of this chapter will be your ability to transform understanding of how to initiate, maintain, and terminate a helping relationship into demonstrated competence to do so.

Relationship

As implied in chapter 1, the helping process takes place in a relationship. Within formal contexts, this relationship takes the form of an interview, a structured helping relationship in which usually only two persons are involved. The variables contributing to the relationship are sketched in Figure 4.

The helping relationship is dynamic, meaning that it is constantly changing at verbal and nonverbal levels. The relationship is the principal process vehicle for both helper and helpee to express and fulfill their needs, as well as to mesh helpee problems with helper expertise. Relationship emphasizes the *affective* mode, because relationship is commonly defined as the inferred emotional quality of the interaction.

Opening an Informal Relationship

Inexperienced helpers often approach a relationship with some anxiety. If you haven't thought much about this topic before, it would be productive to imagine yourself being interviewed and note the qualities the interviewer exhibited to start the relationship off well. While it is difficult to make general rules about opening a helping relationship, the following guidelines should help to ease the first minutes of that first contact.

FIGURE 4. THE HELPING RELATIONSHIP IN THE INTERVIEW

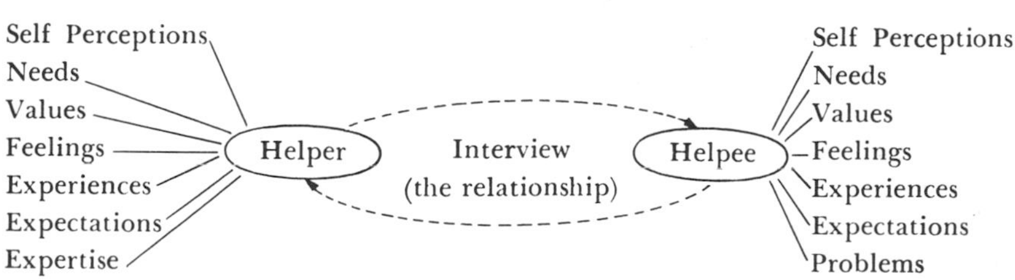

1. *Hello.* A *greeting* of some kind is a suggested natural starter since it affirms the presence and acknowledges the worth of the other person. A pleasant greeting also begins the relationship on grounds familiar to the helpee.

2. *Why Are You Here?* If the contact is helpee initiated, he or she will begin usually by saying why your help is sought. If the helpee does not start, then a simple request to "Tell me why you are here" suffices. If the contact is helper initiated, a brief and honest statement about why you wanted to see the person is all that is required, although reticent helpees may need more encouragement to talk. Suggestions along this line follow later in this chapter under stages of the formal interview.

3. *Where Do We Go from Here?* Informal relationships ebb and flow with the natural inclinations of the two persons, although the general goal is to keep the helpee talking about personal concerns with as few questions as posssible from the helper. Helpees are encouraged to move in their own ways and discuss topics they choose while the helper listens actively according to the methods detailed in the next chapter. In the meantime there is only one thought in the mind of the helper: What is going on in this person's world right now? How does this person see his or her life now? This stance aids in achieving the understanding goals of that first contact. Our sincere interest in the helpee's story is a way of showing concern and caring for the other person also.

If the helping relationship shades into a more formal interview, then other considerations need to be faced, such as: What are our goals? What are my obligations and responsibilities to this other person? What is my role as a helper? How much time am I agreeing to give? What is the nature of the helping contract between us? These questions set the stage for the detailed process discussion to follow.

Dimensions

Brammer and Shostrom (1977) list the main dimensions of a helping relationship. One is *uniqueness-commonality.* Helping relationships generally are unique among human interactions. They have common features, yet they are as diverse and complex as the persons involved. An aspect unique to helping relationships, for example, is the helper's unusually extensive acceptance of the helpee. On the other hand, helping relationships have much in common with friendships, family interactions, and ministerial contacts. They are all aimed toward fulfilling basic human needs, and when reduced to their components, look much alike.

Another dimension is the relative amount of *intellectual and emotional content*. A relationship can be primarily an emotional encounter between two people where no words are spoken, or it can be a heavily verbal and intellectual exchange about the helpee's eligibility for services from the helping agency. Helping relationships typically range over the full spectrum of feeling and thinking. Usually there is a progression of emotional involvement that proceeds from an initial level of attraction, to deeper friendship, through increased involvement in a true encounter. This deepest level is characterized by full loving concern for the other's welfare. Thus, the emotional quality of a helping relationship is characterized by several elements: an *empathic* quality, described in chapter 2; a *friendship* where the people involved like each other; a deep *caring* or *loving* quality; and at times, a true *encountering*, which is a mutual act of entering into one another's worlds of personal experience. The intellectual quality of the relationship is characterized by numerous self-dialogues, including thinking about what is happening, deciding what to do next, and wondering about the meaning of this relationship.

An important implication for helpers here is to be aware of the *level* of emotional involvement taking place and the consequences for the helpee of such involvement. The optimum level toward which to strive depends on one's goal. Helpers, on the one hand, can be so detached and intellectual that they are perceived as distant, disinterested, or afraid of feelings. Yet, if helpers allow themselves to become too emotionally involved, they may lose their objectivity and develop relationships such as those experienced by lovers or parents and children. Helpers need to deal comfortably with this paradox of involvement. They need to maintain their objectivity, so they remain in reasonable control of their own feelings and know what is going on in the relationship, yet remain enough of an emotional participant to keep the helpee involved at an appropriate feeling level.

The dimension of *ambiguity-clarity* refers to the perception of the helping relationship as vague or structured. Initial ambiguity allows the helpee to project needs, concerns, and feelings into the relationship without constraint; whereas, if the relationship were structured initially as a precisely focused interview, the helpee would be inclined to respond to the narrowly perceived purposes of the helper. If the relationship were too ambiguous in terms of purpose and identity of the helper, the helpee would be likely to react with considerable anxiety, or would drift into social conversation. The key to resolving this dilemma is that the helper and helpee must decide what this helping relationship is designed to accomplish and choose a level of ambiguity consonant with this purpose. If the purpose, for example, is to explore helpee feelings or to discover what is on the helpee's agenda, leave the relationship and your helper role deliberately ambiguous so that the helpee can use the relationship as a screen on which to project his or her feelings, ideas, and goals.

A crucial relationship dimension is that of *trust-distrust.* Helpees are willing generally to accept help from people they trust. For trust to develop, helpees must have confidence in their helpers and must be able to believe what they say. Certain specific helper behaviors, such as clear motives for helping, create trust. The motives of the helper must be apparent and attractive to the helpee, and they must not be a cover for helper efforts to control, manipulate, or punish. Under conditions of trust helpees perceive themselves as being accepted and valued people. They feel warmly received. They perceive their helpers as sincere in their efforts to give of themselves and their willingness to reveal their own feelings honestly. The helpee experiences the relationship as a shared and confidential effort to achieve growth, as a mutual problem-solving and learning activity. Yet, the helpee feels free to accept or reject the relationship and the implied help.

Conversely, distrust often causes the helpee to reject offers of help, as when the helpee thinks the helper wants to change him or her. The helpee may feel dependent, inferior, helpless, or depreciated, and thus resist the helper. These reactions become a circular series of events, since helpers sense this resistance and feel unappreciated and possibly even rejected. The helper may then attempt more intensive, but veiled, retaliatory efforts to change the helpee, or may cool, and eventually end, the relationship, with residual feelings of disappointment or anger in both persons. One of the most insidious guises for helping another person is the rationalization that the helper is acting for the helpee's own good, whereas in reality he or she is doing it for manipulative or punitive reasons to fulfill the helper's own needs.

Although little research has been done on trust, two studies have given us a clearer picture of the nature and effect of trustworthiness. Strong and Schmidt (1970) studied the effect of perceived trustworthiness on the helper's influence. They used interviewers trained in trustworthy and untrustworthy behaviors. Trustworthy behavior was defined as showing genuine interest in the helpee as well as absence of ulterior motives, nonconfidentiality, and boastfulness. It was difficult to produce roles characteristic of significant untrustworthy and trustworthy behavior in this study, but they did clarify the nature of the trusting process. In later research Kaul and Schmidt (1971) studied the factors influencing perceptions of trustworthiness. They found that interviewer manner had a more significant impact on perceived trustworthiness than words. The key implication for our discussion of the trust dimension here is that we must attend more to the effects of our nonverbal communication. What we say with our bodies is related to our genuineness and honesty. Kaul and Schmidt's definition of a trustworthy person was one who respects needs and feelings, offers information and opinions for the helpee's benefit, generates feelings of comfort and willingness to confide, and is open and honest about his or her motives. Trust also came from the positive reputation of the helper.

There are other dimensions related to levels of personal-social responsibility, freedom-control, and ethical commitment, but these have been discussed in earlier chapters. This section is an introduction to some general dimensions and relationship problems. The following discussion will describe, in more specific terms, two additional conceptual schemes for understanding the helping process. The first is an overview of the process as experienced typically by both helpee and helper. The second will list the specific stages in a typical model of the helping process.

THE HELPING PROCESS AS EXPERIENCED

The following sequence of events is typical of helpers' and helpees' experiences of moving from first contact through final outcomes. This general sequence is not dependent on helping style or theory of helping; it is an unfolding of a natural process of problem solving. Note that in Figure 5, the helpee's feelings, questions, and interpretations of what is going on are paralleled by those of the helper. The process moves typically from an *initial statement* of a problem by the helpee, to a covert translation of that problem into a broad awareness of the *underlying message.* Then the helpee moves to a further translation of the problem into a desired *goal,* on to an awareness of need for a *problem-solving process,* to experiencing the helper's *strategy* and *method* for reaching the goal or solving the problem. Finally, the helpee experiences the *outcomes* themselves. This sounds like a complicated process, but it is a natural movement toward a goal, fulfilling a need, or solving a problem. The helper goes through a parallel process of experiencing *initial questions,* then forming some preliminary *inferences* and *hypotheses* about what is going on. Making working *agreements* with the helpee follows. Finally, the helper chooses a *strategy* of helping, and moves toward the *outcomes.*

FIGURE 5. THE HELPING PROCESS AS EXPERIENCED BY HELPER AND HELPEE

Phase 1: Building the Helping Relationship

HELPEE BEHAVIOR

Initial statement of concern.

How do I state my desire for help?

"I need help. . . ."

"I have a problem. . . ."

"I'm unhappy. . . ."

"Something is wrong. . . ."

"I can't perform. . . ."

"I can't decide. . . ."

Can I trust this other person?

What am I getting myself into?

Initial statement translated into a basic message.

I can't cope with the demands of myself, of others, of the situation.

I need more information, more skill, more love, more understanding . . . .

HELPER BEHAVIOR

Initial questions and reactions.

Why is the helpee here?

How does the helpee see his or her present situation?

What is the helpee feeling and thinking?

How am I and this relationship perceived?

What is the helpee's world like?

What does the helpee want of me?

Formulating inferences, hunches, and hypotheses.

What messages is the helpee trying to convey?

I see the basic problem as . . . . Is this valid?

Can I meet the helpee's expectations?

What additional information do I need to explore?

HELPEE BEHAVIOR

Statement of a goal (usually in the form of "I want . . ." statements).

I want to decide. . . . do. . . . plan . . . .

I want to feel more confident. . . . worthy. . . . happy . . . .

I want others to like me . . . . notice me . . . . change to . . . . get off my back . . . .

Awareness of process needs.

I want a relationship to explore my feelings.

I want specific information about . . . .

I want to talk over my various choices . . . .

I want more choices to consider . . . .

HELPER BEHAVIOR

Preliminary inferences and judgments about helpee need.

The helpee needs a process—planning, problem solving, decision making.

The helpee needs a relationship to work through feelings or obtain support.

The helpee needs information.

The helpee needs referral for specialized help.

Making an agreement or contract to meet helpee expectations.

I will (can)—
- give information.
- give time to listen.
- give support.

I will not (cannot)—
- relate to this person.
- meet his or her expectancies.

I expect the helpee to—
- do his or her agreed part.
- take responsibility for any decisions or plans.

Phase 2: Facilitating Positive Action

HELPEE BEHAVIOR	
Experience helper's strategy and methods. I meet with the helper for the agreed purposes. I experience what we are doing as helpful (or not helpful) as evidenced by	*Outcomes experienced.* I feel better about myself. I feel better about others. My skills have improved. I feel better about my situation. I enrolled in . . . . I obtained a job as . . . . I experienced myself as competent in . . . .

HELPER BEHAVIOR	
Choosing a strategy of helping. I choose specific interviewing methods to meet helpee needs. I look for feedback from the helpee on the effectiveness of my help. *Looking for evidence of achieving helping goals.* I see progress toward helpee goals. I plan for termination of this helping relationship.	*Outcomes perceived.* I experience myself as helpful to this person. I see specific behaviors the helpee has learned, courses of action he or she has chosen, or plans he or she has made. I hear stated feelings he or she has experienced.

STAGES IN THE HELPING PROCESS

The stages listed below are typical of the process in the two basic phases—relationship and action. They do not always exist in this exact sequence, nor are all stages always present, since helpees typically determine the sequence and length of stages. Some helpees, for example, come with very vague requests, sometimes just with an uncomfortable feeling; whereas others come with specific requests, thoughtful expectations, and much experience. Some help takes the form of specific skill development, such as relaxation. Other help takes a more cognitive form—acquiring information, making a decision, solving a problem, or forming an educational and career plan. Often help is requested for managing intense feelings or resolving interpersonal problems. These diverse helpee needs and problem statements, therefore, call for some variation in the stages.

Another variable determining the sequence and emphasis given the stages in the helping process is the theoretical outlook of the helper. If helpers take a strongly behavioral stance, as described in chapter 7, they will construe the process quite differently from the way a gestalt helper would conceive it. The helper leaning in the behavioral direction would see the process as discovering the problem, establishing the behavioral objectives, describing the interventions, managing the environment, evaluating the behavior change, and following up. The gestalt approach to process, by contrast, focuses on establishing the relationship, expanding awareness and self-support by use of confrontational methods, and enabling the helpee to decide on a course of action growing from the awareness of self and others. Both views emphasize the outcome of personal responsibility for decisions; but the behavioral view stresses the process of managing the external environment, whereas the gestalt and similar views emphasize the process of changing the internal environment (awareness).

From a generalist point of view, there are eight stages contained in the two basic phases of the helping process:

Phase 1: Building Relationships

1. Entry: Preparing the helpee and opening the relationship.
2. Clarification: Stating the problem or concern and reasons for seeking help.
3. Structure: Formulating the contract and the structure.
4. Relationship: Building the helping relationship.

Phase 2: Facilitating Positive Action

5. Exploration: Exploring problems, formulating goals, planning strategies, gathering facts, expressing deeper feelings, learning new skills.
6. Consolidation: Exploring alternatives, working through feelings, practicing new skills.
7. Planning: Developing a plan of action using strategies to resolve conflicts, reducing painful feelings, and consolidating and generalizing new skills or behaviors to continue self-directed activities.
8. Termination: Evaluating outcomes and terminating the relationship.

You may note that the above sequence is a general model of the helping process designed to incorporate problem-solving, skill development, life planning, and awareness models. Because case examples help to make this process explicit and more meaningful, I suggest you extend your imaginings of the opening relationship, described earlier, to a more extended helping relationship. Either imagine a person with whom you have worked, or consider yourself as a former or present helpee, and think through the process steps described above. How does your situation match this sequence of phases and steps?

How would you conceptualize this helping process to fit your personal situation or work setting?

Stage 1: Preparing and Entry

Readiness. The goals of this stage are to open the interview with minimal resistance, lay the groundwork of trust, and enable helpees to state their requests for help comfortably and clearly. Helpees come to a helping relationship with mixed feelings. On the one hand, they want whatever the helper has to offer; yet there is a strong resistance in even the most highly motivated helpees. Basically, people fear to change, and a helping relationship may intensify this fear.

Resistance is a standard term in counseling literature used to denote helpees' defensive reluctance to begin a helping relationship as well as their covert thwarting of the goals of the interview, once the process is underway. There are several reasons for this resistance. In the first place, cultural norms in certain segments of American society construe seeking help as an expression of weakness or incompetence. People are expected to handle their problems with fortitude and common sense, and this cultural pressure to be independent discourages involvement.

Our tendencies to resist change in our style of living create further resistance to the relationship. We talk glibly about growth and becoming more effective people, but we really do not want to work up to our potential by going through the fearful discomfort of change. The following interview excerpt illustrates these points.

Hr: You seem to be just sitting there. What is that doing for you?

He: Well, I can't seem to get going. I don't want to work today.

Hr: You don't really want to help yourself, then?

He: Well, yes I do, honestly, but then again, I'm scared.

Fear of confronting our feelings is a strong deterrent for seeking help. The pain must be great in most of us before we will admit that we need a helping relationship. We may try all kinds of substitutes like drugs, for example, first. It is important for helpers to recognize this ambivalent, or mixed, feeling in all helpees.

We must recognize also that even those who have made a clear commitment to seek a helping relationship use all kinds of stratagems, of which they are unaware, to resist changing. This process also takes place long after the helping relationship is underway. Helpers constantly need to devise methods for dealing with resistance, such as confronting helpees with their behavior, as in the dialogue above.

Helpees may, for example, discuss matters at a high intellectual level to resist facing their feelings.

Helpers frequently ignore the milder forms of resistance, since these forms are protection for the helpee against intense feeling experiences. As the trust level develops, however, resistance tends to diminish. Helpers, therefore, need to focus on building the trust level of their interviews and must ask what in their own behavior might be contributing to helpee resistance.

Think for a moment about relationships in which you were the helpee. What was it like for you to ask for help? What did you feel? Was it easy or hard? What factors enabled you to overcome your resistance? Now think about the present prospects of going to a helping service. What are you experiencing? List the reasons why you would not want to get involved. This experience will provide a basis for understanding the nature of resistance.

The helper should realize some of the realities of a new relationship:

1. It is not easy to receive help.
2. It is difficult to commit one's self to change.
3. It is difficult to submit to the influence of a helper; help is a threat to esteem, integrity, and independence.
4. It is not easy to trust strangers and to be open with them.
5. It is not easy to see one's problem clearly at first.
6. Sometimes problems seem too large, too overwhelming, or too unique to share them easily.

To assist helpees to determine their readiness for a helping relationship, helpers need to remind themselves that before a helping process can begin effectively, the following conditions in the helpee need to prevail:

1. Awareness of feelings of distress.
2. Desire for a change from the present situation or behavior. (They want to help themselves.)
3. Awareness of the potentials and limitations of a helping relationship.
4. Voluntary desire to see a helper.

Setting. The setting has something to do with ease of starting a relationship. This is an individual matter and should be an honest reflection of helper style. The clothes of the helper, the appearance and decor of the room, and the opening conversation should reflect the helper's nature and style. Most helpers agree with the obvious suggestion that distractions and interruptions should be eliminated, but here again, helping can take place anywhere. The traditional formal office may even be a detriment, although it is a common setting for many helping relationships.

Even the distance of the chairs, assuming the helping is conducted while sitting, should be such that it facilitates communication and comfort. Distance between chairs generally varies during the interview depending on the involvement and comfort felt by the participants. Some work best "eyeball to eyeball," whereas other helpees are threatened by close physical proximity. They need the "safety" of a few feet of space. Although these are comparatively trivial considerations, the helper needs to perceive the implications of the setting for accomplishing the goals of the interview.

Opening. Beginning helpers report that opening an interview sometimes makes them apprehensive. Assuming that the helpee initiates the process, a relaxed expectant attitude on the helper's part usually enables helpees to state their reasons for coming or what they feel to be important at the moment. If helpees have difficulty expressing themselves, simple indirect leads are helpful, such as "Please tell me what's on your mind," "What did you wish to discuss with me?" or "I'm interested in knowing where you're at; please fill me in." Note that the lead is vague so as to allow helpees to pick it up any way they wish. Do not imply that they have a "problem" or that they have come into some kind of clinical setting where they are expected to act in a certain way. In less formal helping situations, even more natural conversational openers would be effective. When the helper has initiated the interview, an honest opening statement regarding why the person was asked to come is appropriate. More ideas on starting relationships are presented under leading skills in chapter 4.

Stage 2: Clarification

The goals of this stage are to clarify helpee statements of why they want help and to get a better feel for how helpees see their problems and general life situations. It is not necessary to assume that all helpees come with defined "problems," a general descriptive term for helpee concern.

Use of Questions. It is a common tactical error of helpers at this point to begin asking questions. Helpees often feel interrogated, and as a result, threatened. They may perceive this interview as a problem-solving session, such that if all the facts were brought out, the solutions would be apparent or forthcoming from the wisdom of the helper. Asking questions reinforces the kind of "help set" that physicians model when symptoms and complaints are described to them. Physicians usually offer a diagnosis after such elaborate questioning. The history and diagnoses are followed with suggestions and prescriptions. Our goal in psychological help is to discourage this passive-receptive set, by resisting the temptation to ask many questions and mainly by active listening and by reflecting the feelings expressed by the helpee. We try to suspend judgments and to limit diagnostic thinking, especially in the early stages, although as indicated in the experience list of Figure 5, the helper is thinking about the experiential world of the helpee and is trying to get into his or her perceptual framework much of the time. *Diagnosis* is an important step in some kinds of specialized helping with very disturbed people, but within the framework of helping described in this book it has no place.

The helper encourages helpees to elaborate and clarify their statements about the nature and kinds of help they seek. This process is not belabored, however, because helpees often do not know *why* they want help. Frequently, they are aware only of some behaviors that make them uncomfortable, ineffective, angry, or anxious. Sometimes they are aware only of vague feelings of discomfort. It is not fruitful, therefore, to ask "why" questions, even though this tactic is tempting. It is so easy, for example, to engage in a questioning routine around "Why do you feel this way? Why did you do that? Why don't you try . . . ?" It is more productive to keep helpees focused on both feeling and cognitive levels by dealing with "what" questions, for example, "What are you feeling right now? What is going on in you? What did you do?" usually are productive questions that keep the helpee exploring his or her thoughts.

"How" questions can also help clarify issues. For example, the helper might say, "How does that suggestion help?" "How do you feel right now about this interview?" "How does your wife's behavior affect you?" Helpees can amplify such topics in their own way and clarify and focus their responses at the same time.

Ownership of Problems. Another consideration at this opening level of problem statements is to assist helpees in determining who "owns" the problem. Is the problem that of the helpee exclusively, such as feeling depressed? Is the problem owned by two people involved in a relationship, or does it merely *appear* to belong to two people when it actually belongs to only one of them? For example, a parent may come for help with his or her child. The parent then talks mainly about the child, but actually the parent owns the problem because he or she feels the concern; the child does not. Or perhaps a teacher refers a child to a school counselor "for help." It soon becomes apparent that the teacher is the helpee because he or she has the problem, not the child. Stage 2 goals, then, are to make clear who the principal helpee is and to clarify the helpee's reasons for coming or being referred.

Stage 3: Structure

As helpees explain their reasons for seeking help, or helpers explain why they are offering help, the principal question becomes, What are the conditions under which the relationship will work? The goal for Stage 3 is to decide whether to proceed with the relationship and, if so, on what terms. To reach that goal, the following sequence of questions must be answered, at least tentatively, by the two parties of the helping relationship:

Helper Questions

1. Am I able to work with this person? (skills, knowledge)
2. Do I want to work with this person? (comfort, compatibility)
3. Can I meet his or her expectations? (given my skills and knowledge)
4. What kind of structure do we need to proceed? (informal understanding, counseling contract, leave the issue open)
5. What am I expecting of this person? (time, place, effort, commitment, responsibility)

Helpee Questions

1. Is this a person I can trust?
2. Will this person be helpful on my terms?
3. What will the terms be?
4. Will this relationship get me more involved than I want to be?
5. Am I willing to commit myself to a relationship agreement on the other's terms, or will we work it out together?
6. If I agree to a "contract" to do specific things, can I get out if I want to?

Stage 3 structures vary considerably in complexity and formality; however, most helping relationships take place at a very informal level where either person may withdraw easily at any time. Neither person has a very firm commitment to the other, as in casual friendships.

People handling crisis center phones and interviews, for example, do not quibble about the niceties of relationship building. They deal with the current crisis. Structuring questions such as the above are worked out later if a relationship is indicated. Helpers who take their work seriously feel the need for more commitment and structure, yet they want to maintain a close informal relationship with the helpee. Most helpers, therefore, engage in a process called *structuring.*

Structuring Procedure. Structuring defines the nature, limits, and goals of the prospective helping relationship. During this process the roles, responsibilities, and possible commitments of both helpee and helper are outlined. The helper generally indicates the steps to reach the helpee's goals so that both have a clearer idea of where they are going and about how long it will take. This does not mean that the process is planned and that it is precisely predictable, but there are enough general principles and fairly predictable stages for helping relationships to give helpers a rough idea. Helpees should know where they are (type of agency and type of help offered), who the helper is (qualifications, limitations), and why they are there (purpose of the interview). If these points are not made clear in the referral process, the agency brochures, or the opening comments of Stage 1, they need to be faced before proceeding.

One view of structuring indicates that structure is implicit and that it evolves naturally; therefore, it need not be discussed formally. Helpers must develop their own styles, and they must be flexible in adapting to different helpee circumstances. The main point here is that attention must be paid to the understanding of why this particular helping relationship exists. Lack of such structure may precipitate unnecessary anxiety in the helpee because the relationship is too ambiguous. On the other hand, the anxiety level of the helper may be so high that a compulsive need to structure frequently for his or her own security is felt.

Some of the advantages of agreements on structure are that the *time* to be spent will be clear, both for the first interview and for the total process. Any *fees* involved should be frankly discussed at this stage. *Action limits* can be discussed when an incident takes place. In working with young children, for example, it may be necessary to point out that they can attack the toys or say anything they wish, but they cannot attack the people present. *Role limits* are usually discussed in the early stages because roles may be contradictory. One may offer help unconditionally on the one hand, yet one may exercise some kind of judgmental authority over the helpee on the other hand. An example is the teacher who is often in the position of helper, but who also exercises authority over the students. Many agency workers who administer public programs are in similar positions. Without making a big point of this issue, it is important that these conflicting roles be made clear to helpees. If the helper is a professional, it is not productive to discuss details about differences and similarities among the helping professions, unless there seems to be some crucial misunderstanding. An example would be perceiving the helper as possessing a medical degree when he or she does not have such credentials.

Process Structure. An additional element of structuring that takes place usually in Stage 3 is called *process structure.* If help is to proceed efficiently and constructively, helpees must accept their share of responsibility for the interview, and they must know how to express themselves in a manner that allows the helper to be most effective. In other words, they must *learn* how to be good helpees. Examples of such process values and norms are that present feelings are important data to bring out, that talking about one's self freely and honestly is expected and accepted, that taking responsibility for any choices and actions is necessary, and that although the interview may start on a vague and ragged note, things become more specific and clear as the interview progresses. Much of this process structure comes out naturally from events in the interview and much comes from the helper's effective modeling of these behaviors. The exact form of these process norms depends largely on the helper's theoretical view of the helping process—again a reason for considering seriously one's own theory. The nature and timing of structuring is a controversial issue among helpers. The range of possible views has been presented here so helpers can experiment and develop the style most effective for them.

Formal Contracts. Helpers inclined toward a more behavioral approach to the helping process speak of a formal event in Stage 3, called the *contract.* This is an agreement between the helper and helpee that they will work toward certain *goals,* that each will carry out specific *responsibilities* to achieve the goals, and that certain specific *outcomes* will be taken as evidence that the help was successful. An example is the helpee who sees his or her problem as one of making a career change. The helpees agree to seek certain kinds of information, to keep a log of homework on planning, and to consider the helping process successful when they arrive at three options for choice with confirming and limiting data for each choice. In a more interpersonal problem area, such as excessive shyness, a helpee may agree to spend about ten hours with the helper and follow a prescribed set of exercises possibly involving relaxation methods, trying assertive social behaviors, and agreeing to make two new acquaintances each week. The helping interviews then are devoted to discussing the helpee's feelings about the homework tryouts, learning new skills, revising goals, and looking at evidence of progress. Chapter 6 includes more detail on contracting techniques.

Stage 4: Relationship

The discussion above on structure and contracts assumes that the decision has been made to give a formal helping relationship an extended test. The goal of Stage 4 is to increase the depth of the relationship and the intensity of helpee commitment. It is understood clearly that either the helper or the helpee may bring up the possibility of terminating the relationship by mutual agreement. Stages 1 through 3 usually take place in the first contact so that helpees know when they leave what will happen next and what is expected of them if the relationship is to continue. During this time also increasing trust and openness have deepened the relationship, as described under Stage 1. By the end of Stage 4, the relationship should be firmly established and the helpee should be ready to work specifically toward goals announced upon his or her arrival and as clarified and amplified in Stages 2 and 3.

Silence. The function of the pause, or silence, is of concern at all stages; but it is of particular significance in the relationship and exploratory stages. Pauses have many meanings that require different handling. Helpees may stop talking as a *resistive* act because they don't feel comfortable about revealing themselves further. The trust level may not be sufficiently strong, as indicated by awkward glancing about, flushing, and abrupt changes of topic. If this hunch turns out to be valid, then further discussion of the relationship between helper and helpee is indicated.

A pause may mean the helpee is temporarily *stopped* in the ongoing exploration. Helpees appear preoccupied with their thoughts and sometimes distressed, mainly because they feel blocked in their desire to go on. They may need some quiet time alone to pull their feelings together before they explore further. This is often a very productive time, and the most helpful thing to do is to wait quietly until the helpee is ready to go on. Sometimes, inner struggles take place during these silent periods which may last several minutes; occasionally the helpee will emerge with a significant insight or expression of feeling.

A pause may mean the helpee has come to the *end of a thought* or discussion unit. Typical tapes of helping interviews are characterized by these natural pauses, much like conversation. The helper and helpee then work out a new topic direction. The helpee, for example, may mention several things on his or her mind, and the helper responds with silence or attention to one item, thus starting a new topic. The helper's attention has a rewarding effect that encourages the helpee to explore that new topic further. The helper may suggest several possibilities from which the helper chooses. Usually this is a natural process with attention by both helper and helpee to the nonverbal cues of the other.

Stage 5: Exploration

In this working stage the helper becomes more active and assertive. During the first stages helpers are attempting, through listening, clarifying, and structuring methods, to understand how their helpees see themselves and their worlds. The helpee has been taking the lead. By Stage 5, the helper has a more clear grasp of who the helpee is, what is wanted, and how help can be given. There are two key questions at this exploration stage: What changes in helpees' behavior are appropriate and needed to achieve their goals? What strategies for intervention will most likely produce these outcomes? The term *intervention* is used commonly in formal helping circles to designate techniques that helpers initiate.

What is done at this stage and beyond is tailored to the kind of problem the helpee brings, whether primarily planning, problem solving, interpersonal conflict, or intrapersonal feeling problems. The methods of intervention described in the following chapters are designed to give the helper a wide spectrum of skills and strategies that can be applied selectively to specific helpee problems and expected outcomes. The specific *process goals* for the helper at this exploratory stage, however, are as follows:

1. Maintain and enhance the relationship (trust, ease, safety).
2. Deal with feelings in helper and helpee that interfere with progress toward their goals.
3. Encourage the helpee to explore problems or feelings further (clarify, amplify, illustrate, specify), so helpee's self-awareness is expanded.
4. Encourage helpees to clarify and further specify their goals.
5. Gather necessary facts that will contribute to the solution of helpees' problems.
6. Decide to continue or terminate the relationship.
7. Teach skills required to reach helpee goals (demonstrating, modeling, coaching).
8. Initiate helpee homework activities that move them toward their goals (tryout, evaluation, progress).

In the exploratory stage helpees tend to turn inward while describing feelings and delineating problems. This tendency is expected, but the helpee should understand that exploration of feelings and problems is primarily a prelude to *action* for the consolidation and planning stages. Here helpees move outside of themselves once again toward putting their expanded awareness and new insights into action plans. It is a phase described by Carkhuff and Berenson (1967) as "emergent directionality."

Sometimes helpees feel so good after the exploratory stage that they think their problems are solved. Some helpers think this is the time to terminate, and it may well be an appropriate time; but this may merely be a good feeling or relief of tension with no specific behavior change in sight. This condition is a critical point in a helping relationship.

Another critical point in the exploratory stage is when helpees who are involved in extensive exploration of their feelings experience discouragement. They may want to terminate the relationship out of sheer exhaustion and disillusionment with the process. At this point discussion of their feelings is appropriate, followed by several options: (1) reduce the intensity of exploration by moving to another topic; (2) continue exploring feelings in greater depth; (3) terminate exploration with this helper and consider rebuilding a relationship with another. The third option is especially appropriate when the helper's discomfort with intensive feelings becomes apparent.

Another issue is how assertive helpers should be. In the early stages helpers usually are fairly unassertive, and they encourage helpees to explore on their own initiative. Helpee responsibility for the direction and content of the interview is emphasized by helpers of all theoretical views and styles. As the process lengthens and moves closer to the planning and action stages, helpers generally become more active partners and use all their helping skills.

Transference and Countertransference Feelings. As a result of increasing intensity of interaction, helpees experience specific feelings toward helpers that they may have felt only vaguely in the early stages. These feelings range widely from admiring and affectionate to angry and rejecting. Some reactions may be due to specific behaviors of the helper, but it is more likely that a condition called *transference* is taking place. This reaction is a common event in all human relationships where feelings once felt toward someone close to us are now projected to the immediate helper. Examples are feelings about a parent carried over from childhood. Helpees may see their fathers symbolically in the helper, who now has a position of some authority and power, and they may respond to the helper in the same way they responded to their fathers in earlier years.

We are unaware, of course, that transference is likely explanation for our feelings. Unless this phenomenon is understood and discussed, much effort is expended that is not related to the problem at hand. A frank discussion of authority problems growing out of the present relationship between the helper and helpee could become a growth experience; helper judgment and the specific goals for the particular relationship affect how transference problems are dealt with. When discussing a planning problem with a helpee, for example, it would be inappropriate to spend the limited time talking about transference feelings. It is important to realize, however, that they exist.

A similar condition takes place in the helper who may see the helpee as an ungrateful child, for example. Helpers too may be unaware of the source of their own feelings of annoyance or discomfort with this helpee. They may get sleepy, have difficulty attending, tighten up, sympathize with the helpee, or become argumentative. In the helper these are known as *countertransference* feelings, which have origins similar to those of transference feelings.

To understand countertransference events I suggest you take some time here to recall incidents when you were talking with or interviewing another person. What in your behavior surprised or embarrassed you, such as lapses of attention or yawning? Of course, you may have been very fatigued, but way at that moment and with that person? What happened outside the interview to remind you of that person, such as dreaming about him or her? In severe form we may want to avoid other people who make demands on us. Sometimes this is called "burnout"—when we just cannot talk with another person who wants to be helped. What signs do you note in yourself to indicate that you may be reaching this point? Read on for ideas on what helpers can do about these normal feelings toward helpees.

The important question is not whether countertransference occurs, but what helpers can do about it. If they view these behaviors as signals of unresolved difficulties in their own lives, they can take care of the matter by discussing this possibility briefly with the helpees, so they know at least that the problem resides more in the helper than in their relationship. This honesty should help to resolve some emotional difficulties in the present relationship. For the long term, however, such helpers should think about a personal growth experience for themselves to expand their own awareness and to change their behaviors. Discussing the matter with colleagues is one possible solution. Studying video tapes of one's work with the help of a colleague, and reflecting on what one sees there, is another. Finally, a personal counseling or encounter group experience where helpers can explore their feelings, obtain feedback on their behavior, and try out new forms of responding, may be an answer.

Helping, especially in its more formal aspects of counseling and psychotherapy, is a powerful interpersonal influence process. Strong's studies (1968) showed that helpers who present themselves as attractive and trustworthy experts are much more influential with helpees than those who do not present themselves as experts. Helpers, in turn, react in a variety of ways when helpees treat them as influential experts. Since you, as a helper, must be aware of your style of response on this issue, it would be productive to stop at this point and get in touch with your views on "expertise." How do you respond to experts in any field when you choose to consult them? Identify your basic feelings about experts and authorities. How do you respond when others treat you as an expert? Identify your basic feelings about being treated as an expert. To what extent do you judge your self-inventory as facilitative or nonfacilitative in a helping relationship?

Stage 6: Consolidation

Whereas the bulk of the helping time usually is spent in the work of Stage 5, the task of settling on alternative choices and plans or of practicing the new skills is an important part of the helping process. That inevitable point comes where helpees must *decide* or *act* and stop talking about themselves, their problems, or their possible plans. This consolidation stage flows from the exploratory and blends into the planning stage to follow, but its distinctive process goals are to further clarify feelings, pin down alternative actions, and practice new skills.

Occasionally helpees are so committed to their tasks and have been through the exploratory stages so many times before that they move quickly to the consolidation and planning stages. In such cases, the bulk of the time is spent in decision making and planning. This brief description of the consolidation, planning, and action stages compared to the more elaborate explanation of issues at earlier stages in no way diminishes their importance or time priority.

Stage 7: Planning

This stage is characterized by rational planning processes where plans for termination and continuing alone are formulated. The process goals for this stage are to crystallize discussions of earlier stages into a specific plan of action and to decide that growth has proceeded to the point where termination of the relationship is indicated. Any tag ends of feelings are worked through, and bringing up new topics with feelings is discouraged. In helping processes that are heavily cognitive, such as career-planning interviews, this stage becomes quite lengthy since many action steps to accomplish the plan need to be formulated. For example, schools need to be contacted and application papers completed.

Discussions of Stages 6 and 7 have been comparatively brief since the strategies and methods most used in these stages are presented in chapters 4 through 6.

Stage 8: Termination

In this stage the accomplishments are summarized. Usually a general evaluation of what was accomplished in light of the goals takes place. If the goals were not achieved, hypotheses as to why they were not realized are made.

A relationship can be terminated in many ways, and helpers must develop their individual techniques. Summarizing the process as indicated above is one effective method. A helpful procedure is to ask the helpee to summarize. If a number of plans were made or steps decided, a written summary developed jointly will help. Keeping the conversation at an intellectual level tends to discourage further exploration of feeling. If the process has involved several interviews, then *spreading* the last couple of contacts over a longer time span will tend to de-escalate the involvement. Reference to the agreed *time limits* along with the summary facilitates termination. *Referral* may be indicated if the helpee feels a sense of incompleteness and the helper is reluctant to continue the relationship. Leaving the door open for possible *follow-ups* may make the termination less abrupt. Frequently in agencies like schools, the helper may want to maintain a kind of *standby* relationship to observe and occasionally facilitate the helpee's further development.

Leave-taking is not the problem that is usually anticipated if the stages discussed above have unfolded satisfactorily. There is a natural awareness that "This is the end." Helpees usually are eager to leave since they feel good about their new autonomy, plans, or solutions. Occasionally they even harbor some feelings of resentment (usually projected to the helper) that they needed help in the first place. Feelings of gratitude are expressed sometimes, but the helper should be wary of these since the goal was to have helpees feel that they solved their own problems. To have grateful helpees, though, expands the self-esteem of the helper. Sometimes helpees have lingering dependency feelings expressed as reluctance to leave. They bring up "just one more thing" or prolong the goodbye ceremony excessively. Some helpees literally need to be led out the door.

In this chapter on the helping process a wide range of issues was discussed. Such a chapter presents a dilemma. On the one extreme are those helpers who say the helping process evolves. You do what comes naturally as in developing a friendship; you trust your feelings since there are no specific cognitive guidelines. At the other extreme are those helpers who view the process as a highly structured enterprise that can be described in terms of precise objectives, steps, methodologies, and outcomes. The middle position presented here incorporates elements from diverse theoretical views about the helping process within the context of everyday practical considerations.

Expected Outcomes

You can now: (1) list seven dimensions of a helping relationship; (2) describe and illustrate the general sequence of events in the helping process as the helper and helpee experience these events; (3) identify eight stages in the helping process from entry to termination and cite examples of typical issues that must be faced at each stage. The principal outcome expected is that you have begun to develop your own "cognitive map" of the helping process which is useful to you in facing the numerous issues of facilitating a helping relationship. The final test of your mastery of this chapter is your capacity to demonstrate your ability to initiate, maintain, and terminate a helping relationship that leads to specific helpee goals.

Suggestions for Further Study

Brammer, L., and Shostrom, E., *Therapeutic Psychology: Fundamentals of Actualization Counseling and Psychotherapy.* 3rd ed. Englewood Cliffs, N.J.: Prentice-Hall, 1977. (Ch. 4 on steps and critical points in the counseling process.)

Carkhuff, R., and Berenson, B., *Beyond Counseling and Psychotherapy.* New York: Holt, Rinehart & Winston, 1967. (A model of the counseling process based on facilitative process.)

Corliss, R., and Rabe, P., *Psychotherapy from the Center: A Humanistic View of Change and Growth.* Scranton, Pa.: International Textbook, 1969. (A humanistic view of the process, especially ch. 2 on starting, ch. 5 on growth, ch. 6 on termination.)

Krumboltz, J. D., and Thoreson, C. E., eds., *Counseling Methods.* New York: Holt, Rinehart & Winston, 1976. (A collection of articles on the helping process from a behavioral viewpoint.)

Martin, D., *Learning-based Client-centered Therapy.* Monterey, Ca.: Brooks/Cole, 1972. (An approach to the helping process based on a blend of behavioral and client-centered views.)

Truax, C., and Carkhuff, R., *Toward Effective Counseling and Psychotherapy.* Chicago: Aldine, 1967. (A critique of the helping process on the basis of research findings and practice. Also, an analysis of the effective ingredients in psychotherapy.)

FOUR

Helping Skills for Understanding

This chapter focuses on skills that promote understanding of self and others. These skills fall into seven clusters:

1. Listening skills

Attending—noting verbal and nonverbal behaviors

Paraphrasing—responding to basic messages

Clarifying—self-disclosing and focusing discussion

Perception checking—determining accuracy of hearing

2. Leading skills

Indirect leading—getting started

Direct leading—encouraging and elaborating discussion

Focusing—controlling confusion, diffusion, and vagueness

Questioning—conducting open and closed inquiries

3. Reflecting skills

Reflecting feelings—responding to feelings

Reflecting experience—responding to total experience

Reflecting content—repeating ideas in fresh words or for emphasis

4. Summarizing skills
Pulling themes together
5. Confronting skills
Recognizing feelings in self—being aware of helper experience
Describing and sharing feelings—modeling feeling expression
Feeding back opinions—reacting honestly to helpee expressions
Meditating—promoting self-confrontation
Repeating—tapping obscure feelings
Associating—facilitating loosening of feelings
6. Interpreting skills
Interpretive questions—facilitating awareness
Fantasy and metaphor—symbolizing ideas and feelings
7. Informing skills
Advising—giving suggestions and opinions based on experience
Informing—giving valid information based on expertise

Outcomes You Can Expect

The outcomes you can expect from studying this chapter are competencies to: (1) identify seven helping skills that contribute to self-understanding; (2) cite subskills in each skill cluster and give examples from helping interviews; and, with practice, (3) use seven basic skill clusters effectively in helping relationships.

The final criterion of success will be your demonstrated performance of the skills such that the helpee feels understood and confirms this feeling with appropriate verbal or nonverbal behavior. You may expect helpees to respond positively to you when they feel you understand them. You can expect that they will talk about themselves and you more freely. They will share their new understandings with you. Later, you may expect helpees to try to change themselves or their circumstances on the basis of their new understandings, skills, and changed environments.

Rationale for Skills Training

The skills described here and in Chapters 5 and 6 are based on the idea that by learning the components of a skill, one can then put them together into a complex performance. By looking at specific helping skills we can explain the total interview interaction. This approach, described in more detail in Chapter 7, is known as microskills training and is analogous to skills training in a sport such as golf, in which one learns the fundamental skills of stance, grip, and swing. Research supports the validity of this approach, but the principal problem is putting the components together into a smooth, flowing, and natural performance.

Skill Cluster 1: Listening Skills

At first glance the term *listening* implies a passive act of taking in the content of the helpee's communication, but actually it involves a very *active* process of responding to total messages. It includes not only listening with your ears to helpee words and with your eyes to your helpee's body language, but a total kind of perceptiveness best described by Reik's (1948) phrase "listening with the third ear." It means also that we are silent much of the time and that the helpees talk. When helpers can answer in considerable detail the question, What is going on in this person right now and in his or her life space? they are listening with all their perceptual capacities. Listening skills are basic to all interviewing whether the purpose be for gaining information, conducting structured depth interviews, or helping informally.

Attending

Attending has several components, which have been studied intensively by Ivey and others (1968). It is important initially to emphasize the cultural context of these skills. Each culture, for example, places its own norms and meanings on eye contact and distance: In a Middle Eastern setting eye-to-eye contact is permitted between two men but not between a man and a woman; sustained eye contact is considered offensive to some native American groups; in American culture a comfortable helping distance is three or four feet. The following descriptions of attending skills are based largely on experiences with middle-class Americans and should be adapted to other cultural settings.

The first component we will consider is *contact,* principally through the eye. Looking at other people, usually at their eyes, is a way of indicating intense interest in them, because eyes are one of our key vehicles for communicating. This does not mean that eye contact must be a fixed stare to be effective. If the helper is honestly interested and at ease, he or she will look naturally at the helpee while the person is talking. Simply writing about eye contact does not do justice to the power of the eyes to communicate caring and understanding as well as to maintain attention. Think of your own experience when someone looked at you intensively. Sometimes it was done in a vacuous way just to hold your attention. At other times the person said with his or her eyes in a warm way, "Look at me; I hear you; I understand," so that you felt the person genuinely cared about you and understood how you were feeling. At the same time the helper is picking up nonverbal messages from the helpee's eyes.

Distance between helper and helpee needs experimentation before the most comfortable distance for the two is discovered. Some helpees are very uncomfortable, for example, if the eye contact is less than three feet or so, because they are so socially conditioned against close contact. Helpee nonverbal behavior should be watched for signs of stress or discomfort when eye contact is direct.

A second element of attending is *posture.* Usually, the interested helper leans toward the helpee in a relaxed manner. Relaxation is important because tenseness tends to shift the focus from the helpee to the helper, in addition to provoking an empathic tense response in the helpee.

A third related element of attending is *gesture.* The helper communicates much with body movements. If helpers flail wildly with their hands, or if they cross them over their chests in a rather pontifical manner, they will very likely communicate some unintended messages. Try to be aware of the messages your gestures and posture send to helpees. Are the messages ones you intend to communicate?

The helper's *verbal* behavior, a fourth attending component, relates to what the helpee has said. The helper does not ask questions, take the topic in a new direction, nor add to the helpee's meaning, but the helper might, for example, mention a word or reflect a phrase from the statements of the helpee to focus further on an idea. Some confirming, yet not too personal, comment such as, "I see what you mean," "I can appreciate what you went through," or "That certainly seems to tie things together," often helps to keep helpees exploring and assures them that you are listening.

Why does attending behavior work so well? It is very rewarding according to studies, and helpees like it. The *effect on helpees* of attending behavior is to *encourage* them to verbalize their ideas or feelings freely. It has a powerful *reinforcing effect,* in other words. It allows helpees to explore in their own ways and tends to build a sense of responsibility for the interview. This is one difference between helping and conversation; in social interaction there is more give and take of opinions, questions, and feelings. Conversely, *selective inattention* by the helper can serve to discourage further exploration of the topic. For example, the helpee may be on a rambling intellectual description of an historical event. You may think it more productive to have him focus on how he feels now about that event, so you attend when he focuses on feelings and ignore him when he is on a story-telling trip. You can see how *controlling* attending behavior can be. Helpees control helpers, too, by giving them verbalizations that hold their attention.

If a helper is relaxed, the helpee will tend to be more at ease also. One of the most difficult tasks for the beginning helper is to let helpees tell their stories without profuse questioning and jumping from topic to topic in a tense manner.

Attending behavior, furthermore, is a kind of "fail-safe" method for opening an interview because it furthers the goals of helpee self-exploration and minimizes the chances of making destructive interventions. Even if an awkward silence takes place, the helper can acknowledge what has just been stated or refer to some earlier comments.

The following list is a summary of guidelines for effective attending behavior:

1. Establish *contact* through looking at helpees when they talk.
2. Maintain a *natural relaxed posture* that indicates your interest.
3. Use *natural gestures* that communicate your intended messages.
4. Use *verbal statements* that relate to helpee statements without interruptions, questions, or new topics.

An outline of a simple exercise to learn attending skills is included in Appendix A.

Paraphrasing

Paraphrasing is a method of restating the helpee's basic message in similar, but usually fewer, words. The main purpose of paraphrasing is for helpers to test their understanding of what the helpee has said. (It is a practical test of your attending too!) A second purpose is to communicate to helpees that you are trying to understand their basic message, and if successful, that you have followed their verbal explorations. A paraphrase executed to the helpee's satisfaction is one objective definition of understanding.

The helper translates raw perceptions of what the helpee is saying into more precise wording, repeating only the helpee's message without adding any new ideas. To help in this process helpers should ask themselves constantly, What is this person's basic thinking and feeling message to me? The helper, at the time of a natural break in the flow of ideas and feelings, summarizes concisely what has been expressed. Usually the paraphrase has heavy cognitive content, although it includes feelings if these are an important part of the helpee's message. Helpers should look for some cues that their paraphrasing has been helpful. Examples of paraphrasing are:

He: I really think he is a very nice guy; he's so thoughtful, sensitive, and kind. He calls me a lot. He's fun to go out with.

Hr: You like him very much, then.

He: I do, very much.

He: I just don't understand. One minute she tells me to do this, and the next minute to do that.

Hr: She really confuses you.

He: Yeah, she sure does, and besides. . . .

Paraphrasing is especially helpful in exposing and clarifying the mixed or double message. When people apparently do not want to make a direct statement about feelings, they couch their statements in obscure language. The task of the helper is to pick up the two messages from both verbal and nonverbal cues and restate them in clear form. If this restatement does not result in increased understanding by helpees, then confrontive methods where the discrepancy is pointed out more directly may be appropriate. An example is:

He: I really love my wife. She does many things for me constantly. She looks after my clothes, and she keeps track of where I am all the time because she says she's worried about me.

Hr: You appreciate your wife's attentiveness; but I detect in your tone resentment over the constant attention she is showing.

He: Yes. I have feelings both ways about her attention, I guess.

One problem in using paraphrasing and other listening component skills is that if helpers are not careful, they develop a highly stylized way of responding that may annoy helpees. Helpers may say repeatedly, for example, "I hear you saying. . . ." Paraphrasing seems a bit artificial at first until the helper experiences some encouraging responses from the helpee. After a while it feels like a more natural form of communication than the usual questions, opinions, veiled threats, or bland conversation fillers.

Helpees feel understood as a consequence of paraphrasing. It may clarify their perception of what they have said and give a sense of direction to their rambling statements. Helpees tend to like the helper who paraphrases skillfully. The final effect of paraphrased statements is that helpees feel encouraged to go on. When learning paraphrasing skills in a laboratory setting, students should practice until the "helpees" indicate that the paraphrase is accurate to their satisfaction in at least two out of three trials. Appendix B contains a brief illustrative exercise to learn paraphrasing.

Here is a summary of guidelines for paraphrasing:

1. Listen for the *basic message* of the helpee.
2. *Restate* to the helpee a concise and simple summary of the basic message.
3. Observe a *cue,* or ask for a *response,* from the helpee that confirms or denies the accuracy and helpfulness of the paraphrase for promoting understanding.

Clarifying

Clarifying brings vague material into sharper focus. It goes beyond simple paraphrasing in that the helper makes a *guess* regarding the helpee's *basic message* and offers it to the helpee. A helper also may ask for clarification when he or she cannot make sense out of the helpee's responses. The message may have been so vague, the wording so confusing, the reasoning so circuitous, or the style so complex, that it is a strain to try to paraphrase. Examples of what might follow a rambling helpee monologue are: "I'm confused, let me try to state what I think you were saying." "I lost you there; I'm not clear how you feel about your job; could you give me a brief repeat and an illustration?" "It seems to me you were trying to focus on something there, but the ideas just seemed to tumble over one another." "I'm not sure I understand; could you tell me more?"

This method has a touch of interpreting or explaining how the helper sees the situation, and this interpreting need is one of the strong temptations to which helpers must not submit in the early stage of the relationship. The clarifying remarks are stated in terms of the helper's feelings of confusion to avoid implications of criticism at this tender stage. After all, the confusion may be due to the helper's inattention rather than to confusing helpee statements. Clarifying responses or requests should result in more clear helpee statements, such as efforts to rephrase, to summarize, or to illustrate.

General guidelines for clarifying are:

1. *Admit confusion* about helpee's meaning.
2. Try a *restatement* or *ask for clarification,* repetition, or illustration.

When the intent of helpers is to clarify helpee communications by giving some of their own reactions, the act is often termed *self-disclo-*

sure. Here the helper takes some risks in giving personal reactions to what is going on, but does not do so as strongly or directly as in confrontation methods.

Perception Checking

Perception checking asks helpees to verify your perceptions of what they said, usually over several statements. Ask for feedback about the accuracy of your listening. The reason that perception checking is so effective as a listening skill is that it is a method of giving and receiving feedback on the accuracy of the communication. Assumptions that understanding is taking place are checked out with the helpee. Here again, ordinary social conversation differs from a helping interview. We are conditioned socially to chatter onward, even to deliberately confuse the meaning with innuendo, humor, irony, and metaphor. We rarely check with one another about what we intend to say. In helping relationships we reverse this process and put a heavy premium on direct and clear communication aided by frequent perception checks.

Examples of helper perception checks are: "You seem to be very irritated with me; is that right?" "I was wondering if the plan you chose is the one you really want. You expressed some doubt; did I hear correctly?" "I want to check with you what I'm hearing. You said that you love your wife, yet in the last few minutes, you said that you can't stand to be with her. I detected strong contradictory feelings toward her; is that the way it appears to you too?"

The effect on the helpee is likely to be a feeling of being understood. Listening, followed by perception checking, is a method of clearing up confusing communications quickly. Perception checking thus serves to correct misperceptions of the helper before they increase to misunderstandings.

In summary, guidelines for perception checking are:

1. *Paraphrase* what you think you heard.
2. Ask for *confirmation* directly from the helpee about the accuracy of your perception of what was said.
3. Allow the helpee to *correct your perception* if it was inaccurate.

Listening is the key skill in this cluster. To use it naturally and effectively, helpers must want very much to understand their helpees, to communicate meaningfully with them, and to relate to them with acceptance and trust. Effective listening requires much confidence in helpees' abilities to solve their own problems and to establish their independent identities.

Skill Cluster 2: Leading

The purpose of leading is to encourage the helpee to respond to open communication. Although leading skills are used throughout the helping process, they are useful particularly in the opening stages of a relationship to invite verbal expression. The helper anticipates slightly the helpee's direction of thought as a method for stimulating talk. It is analogous to the football passer who anticipates the receiver's path so that the ball and the receiver arrive at the same point. The helper's interventions thus appear to their helpees appropriate to where they want to go.

Leading sometimes is described in helping literature as the helper's degree of impact on, or thinking ahead of, the helpee. All helping skills can be rated on the amount of leading involved in their use, but for purposes of this discussion, leading will mean the more specific act of anticipating where the helpee is going and the act of responding with an appropriately encouraging remark.

More specific objectives of leading are: (1) to encourage helpees to explore feelings and to elaborate on those feelings discussed already; (2) to allow helpees freedom to explore in a variety of directions and to respond freely to what is going on; and (3) to encourage helpees to be active in the process and to retain primary responsibility for direction of the interview.

Indirect Leading

The main purposes of indirect leading are to get helpees started and to keep responsibility on them for keeping the interview going. One common use of this idea is to open an interview. Examples are: "What would would you like to talk about?" "Perhaps we could start by your telling me where you're at now." "Please tell me why you are here?" Later interview examples are: "Tell me more about that." "You were saying (pause)." "What do you think that means?" "How did you feel?" "Is there anything more you would like to discuss?" The generality of these leads allows helpees to project their own ideas and direction into the interview. Sometimes, pausing and looking expectantly at the helpee serves as an indirect lead.

Helpees recognize indirect leads as invitations to tell their stories or elaborate on what has been said. This lead is encouraging to most helpees, because they experience more responsibility for the relationship. To others it is threatening or annoying since they often expect the expert to be more active and to do most of the talking, advising, and questioning. More ideas for opening interviews are discussed under Stage 1 of the helping process in chapter 3.

The following are guidelines for indirect leading:

1. Determine the *purpose* of the lead clearly.
2. Keep the lead *general* and deliberately vague.
3. *Pause* long enough for the helpee to pick up the lead.

Direct Leading

Direct leading is a method of focusing the topic more specifically. This method also encourages helpees to elaborate, clarify, or illustrate what they have been saying. Sometimes a strong element of suggestion is included. Some examples are: "Tell me more about your mother." "Suppose we explore your ideas about teaching a little more." "How do you mean—funky?" "Can you think of an illustration that happened recently?"

The behavior of helpees in response to a direct lead usually is to comply with the specifics of the lead, particularly if the helper's attitude manifests interest to match his or her words. The main long-range consequence, however, is to enhance helpee awareness and later understanding, through more elaborate exploration of feelings.

The guidelines for direct leading are:

1. Determine the *purpose* of the lead.
2. Express the purpose in words that elicit *specific elaboration*.
3. Allow the helpee *freedom to follow* your lead.

Focusing

Focusing the talk on a topic that the helper thinks would be fruitful to explore is used when the helpee is rambling vaguely. Often in the early stages, helpees will wander over numerous topics, sometimes in circular fashion. Occasionally, the helper's indirect leads have encouraged this wandering which, if allowed to continue for several minutes, tends to become confusing for both. When helpers think that their helpees have explored the main topics of their concern, then the helpers may stop the helpees and ask them to focus on one aspect, since another purpose of focusing is to emphasize a single feeling or idea chosen from a vast array of possible intellectual verbiage. Focusing is also a way of aiding helpees to get in touch with their feelings.

Some illustrations of focusing leads are: "Please elaborate more specifically on those feelings about your mother." "You have been discussing many topics the last few minutes; could you pick the most important one to you and tell me more about it?" "Can you choose one word to describe the last five minutes' talk?" "We have been talking about words, words, words, but I haven't detected much feeling yet; could you name a feeling you have right now?" "What were your feelings as we've been talking?" "Let's not talk for awhile. I suggest you close your eyes and try to get in touch with what you are feeling."

Focusing can sometimes be done by picking out one word or a short phrase from the helpee's talk and repeating it with a question mark or with emphasis. For example, after a helpee has been talking about how confusing her relationships with her supervisor have been, you might say, "Confusing?" The effect is, "Tell me more!" The one word focusing method can be effective in keeping the helpee going. The helper can say, for example, "And?" "Then, what?" or "But?"

Focusing tends to reduce the helpee's confusion, diffusion, and vagueness. Again, the ultimate expected outcome is more meaningful verbalization, and eventually, increased understanding. Another immediate outcome expected from leads focusing on feelings is that the helpee will talk more about her feeling experiences. This skill, like all others in the leading cluster, has a controlling effect on the helpee, so the helper should exert cautious judgment about the degree of his or her leading.

In summary, guidelines for focusing are:

1. Use your *own feelings* of confusion and sense of helpee direction as a guide to decide when to focus.
2. Be alert to *feedback* from the helpee about priority of topics.
3. Assist the helpee to *focus on feelings* that may be hidden in the discussion.

Questioning

Many of the leads described above have been illustrated in the form of open questions that lead the helpee to further exploration. Such questions are not those used to obtain information nor those which can be answered with "yes" or "no." They are open-ended questions that leave helpees free to explore and to take the interview where they wish, rather than into areas of helper interest. This method of questioning assumes that the questions are to assist the helpee to understand rather than to promote the helper's understanding.

An example of an open question is, "Could you explain more about your relationships with your parents?" *not,* "Do you get along well with your parents?" Other examples are: "What do you mean by 'failure'?" "How do they indicate their feelings?" Note that questions beginning with "how" or "what" tend to elicit elaborated responses. The effect is different from those starting with "are," "is," or "do." It would be difficult to answer the above questions with a single helpee "yes" or "no."

The following list summarizes guidelines for questioning leads:

1. Ask *open-ended questions* that cannot be answered with "yes" or "no."
2. Ask questions that elicit *feelings* about what the helpee has just said rather than information.
3. Ask questions that lead to *clarification for the helpee* rather than information for the helper.

Skill Cluster 3: Reflecting

Reflecting is one way of expressing to helpees that we are in their frame of reference and that we affirm their deep concerns. There are three areas of reflecting—feeling, experience, and content. From the helper's viewpoint, the main purpose of using reflection is to understand helpee experience and to tell helpees that we are trying to perceive the world as they do.

Reflecting Feelings

Reflecting feelings involves expressing in fresh words the helpee's essential feelings, stated or strongly implied. The purpose of reflecting feelings is to focus on *feeling* rather than on *content,* to bring vaguely expressed feelings into clearer awareness, and to assist the helpee to "own" his or her feelings. So often helpees talk about their feelings as "it" or "them," as if feelings were not part of themselves. This is why we usually begin the reflecting method with "*You* feel" as an attempt to help him reown the feeling. You will know when your reflection is accurate because the helpee will tend to respond with something like, "Yeah, that's it."

Skillful use of reflecting depends on the helper's ability to identify feelings and cues for feelings, from body cues as well as words. It is inappropriate, generally, to ask directly, "And how does that make you feel?" Most of the time, the answer should be fairly obvious. Helpees will probably respond like Louis Armstrong did when someone asked how to know good jazz—"If you have to ask, you'll never know."

Helpers must themselves experience feelings and be in touch with those feelings. Feelings are more subtle than emotions, such as anger, love, disgust, fear, or aggression. Examples of feelings would be affection, pleasure, hostility, guilt, or anxiety. When a helpee is expressing strong emotion, it is so obvious to both, that reflecting is unnecessary. The more subtle feelings, however, are often disguised behind words. The helper looks for these hidden feelings and enables the helpee to recognize them more clearly.

The English language is notoriously deficient in varied designations for feelings. A productive activity for helpers is to list common feeling words to make them more accessible when helpers are groping for descriptive terms. Imagine a number of emotional situations and brainstorm all the feeling words you can think of. Compare your list with others and compile a common list to broaden your descriptive language. Groups completing this activity frequently come up with over five hundred words describing various shades of feelings.

The steps in reflection of feeling, then, are to determine what feeling the helpee is expressing, to describe this feeling clearly, to observe the effect, and to judge by the reactions of the helpee whether the reflection was facilitative or obstructive. Sometimes, inaccurate reflections can have a facilitative effect, inasmuch as the helpee will often correct the helper and state feelings more clearly. Examples of reflecting feelings are: "In other words, you hate his guts." "You've always wanted to be a doctor." "He makes you feel guilty all the time." "It really hurts to be rejected by someone you love." Sometimes two contradictory (ambivalent) feelings are expressed, and a reflection clarifies this condition as, "He makes you angry when he punishes you, yet you feel relieved about it, too."

Reflecting Experience

This reflection is descriptive feedback that indicates broad observations of the helper. It is done without editorializing, unlike confronting skills, described later, in which the helper tells what he or she thinks about the behavior.

Reflecting experience goes beyond verbalized feelings in that the helper also reads the implied feelings of nonverbal body language. The helper notes, for example, rapidity of speech, heavy breathing, sighing, flushing, changing postures, and darting glances as cues to the helpee's feeling. When reflecting feelings implied in body language, it is a good idea to describe some observed behavior first, then reflect the feeling. Examples are, "You are smiling (behavior description); but I sense you are really hurting inside" (reflection of feeling). "You say you really care about her (description), but almost every time you talk about her you clench your fists (description); it seems you strongly resent her" (interpretation).

Reflecting Content

Reflecting content is repeating in fewer and fresher words the essential ideas of the helpee, and is like paraphrasing. It is used to clarify ideas that the helpee is expressing with difficulty. Helpees lack vocabulary, for example, to express ideas simply and clearly, so reflecting content is a skill to give them words for expressing themselves. Sometimes it helps to repeat a helpee's statement, emphasizing a key word. The helpee says, for example, "His remark really cut me." The helper responds, "It *really* hurt."

In actual practice the three reflecting skills blend into one another. The helper is paying attention to *what* the helpee is saying (content), but also *how* he or she is saying it (feeling tone). Helpers usually respond with a mix of feeling and content to suit their process goals at that moment. They may judge, for example, that the helpee is not ready to face the deeper feelings implied in his or her body language, so they will emphasize content. Reflecting is a way of controlling feeling awareness and expression in the helping interview. On the other hand, in the early stages helpers may wish to emphasize recognition of the total feeling impressions they get from feeling words and observations of body movements and postures.

Helpees experience the reflecting helper as a person who understands what they, the helpees, are experiencing. This favorable reaction increases the possibility that the long range outcomes of understanding self and others will be reached. A more immediate outcome is that helpees will be able to identify and express feelings more effectively. Furthermore, they will be able to own their feelings as indicated by more "I feel" statements. In other words, they will be more ready to continue expressing feelings.

Common Errors in Reflecting

Some common errors in using reflecting methods are, first, *stereotyping* your responses. This means that helpers tend to begin their reflections in the same monotonous way, such as, "You feel," "You think," "It seems to you," "I gather that." This repetitive style gives the impression of insincerity or an impoverished word supply. We thus need to vary our styles of reflecting.

Another error is *timing*. Beginning helpers sometimes get into a pattern of reflecting after almost every statement the helpee makes, or they wait for a long monologue to finish and then try heroically to capture the complex feelings in one statement. It is not necessary to reflect every statement, yet it is effective to interrupt the helpee occasionally to reflect. Usually it helps to nod acceptance or give a slight "uh huh" or "I see," to encourage continuation until a reflection seems appropriate.

Overshooting with too much *depth* of feeling for which the helpee is unprepared may retard the interview. We may read more interpretations into statements than are there. The helpee says, for example, "I don't know if I can stay overseas for a year without her." The helper who reads more depth of feeling than is there might respond, "You feel you can't function at all unless she is with you."

The *language* must be appropriate to the cultural experience and educational level of the helpee. For example, the helpee might say, "I can't make it with girls; I'm so shy." An *in*appropriate helper response would be, "Your inferiority complex really shows with girls then." At the same time the language of reflection must be natural for the helper too. If he or she is a traditional type, for example, the helper would appear as a phony to use "mod" language.

It may be reassuring to realize that helpees usually are not as critical as these illustrations imply. As helpers, we can reflect incorrectly, but if our sincerity and interest shine through, helpees are amazingly tolerant of bungling efforts. Occasionally, an inaccurate reflection will elicit a correcting response from the helpee so that the net effect is clarification and progress even though the reflection was not accurate.

A summary of guidelines for reflecting is as follows:

1. Read the *total message*—stated feelings, nonverbal body feelings, and content.
2. Select the best *mix* of content and feelings to fulfill the goals for understanding at this stage of the helping process.
3. *Reflect* the experience just perceived.
4. *Wait* for helpee's confirming or denying response to your reflection as a cue about what to do next.

Skill Cluster 4: Summarizing

Summarizing skills include attention to *what* the helpee says (content), *how* it is said (feelings), and the *purpose, timing,* and *effect* of the statements (process). Most helping interviews wander widely over many ideas and feelings. This may be part of the helpee's manner of showing discomfort by resisting direct discussion, or of keeping the helper at a safe emotional distance for awhile. It may reflect also the helpee's unwillingness to terminate the interview. Summarizing involves tying together into one statement several ideas and feelings at the end of a discussion unit or the end of an interview. It is much broader, therefore, than paraphrasing a basic message as indicated in the following example. Following a discussion of the helpee's vague feelings of inadequacy the helper says, "From your talk about family, school, and now your new job of selling, you appear to have experienced feelings of personal failure in all of them."

Summaries of an interview, or a series of contacts, may include a long paragraph, but the idea is to pick out the highlights and general themes of the content and feelings. Summaries of *process* include statements of where the helping process has been going and where it is now. The helper may say, for example, "You've been discussing your ideal jobs and what things you have liked and disliked about your past work; you've also talked about your plans for more training. Are you ready to take a look at some other considerations in planning for a new career?"

The main purpose of summarizing is to give the helpee a feeling of movement in exploring ideas and feelings, as well as awareness of progress in learning and problem solving. Summarizing also helps to finish an interview on a natural note, to clarify and focus a series of scattered ideas, and to clear the way for a new idea. It has the effect also of reassuring helpees that you have been tuned in to their messages all along. For the helper it serves as an effective check on the accuracy of perceiving the full spectrum of helpee messages. Summarizing the previous sessions at the beginning of an interview often provides needed continuity.

The helper tries to get helpees to do the summarizing, if possible. This is a test of their understanding as well as a method of keeping responsibility on them. The helper may say, for example, "How does our work look to you at this point? Try to pull it together briefly." "Let's take a look at what we've accomplished in this interview; how does it appear to you?" When a relationship is terminated, summarizing will probably be a joint effort to capture the essential points explored, progress achieved, and next steps planned.

Guidelines for summarizing are:

1. *Attend* to the various *themes* and emotional *overtones* as helpees speak.
2. Put together the key ideas and feelings into *broad statements* of their basic meanings.
3. *Do not add* new ideas to the summary.
4. *Decide* if it would be more helpful to state your summary or ask them to summarize the basic themes, agreements, or plans. In deciding, consider your *purpose:*

Was it to *warm up* helpees at the beginning of the interview?
Was it to *focus* their scattered thoughts and feelings?
Was it to *close* discussion on this theme?
Was it to *check* your understanding of the interview progress?
Was it to *encourage* them to explore themes more completely?
Was it to *terminate* the relationship with a progress summary?
Was it to *assure* them that their interviews were moving along well?

Skill Cluster 5: Confronting

Constructive confrontation involves a complex cluster of helping skills consisting of:

1. *Recognizing* feelings in one's self as a helper.
2. *Describing* feelings in one's self and sharing them with the helpee.
3. *Feeding back* reactions in the form of *opinions* about his or her behavior.
4. *Meditating* as a form of self-confrontation.
5. *Repeating* as a form of emphasizing and clarifying.
6. *Associating* as a method of getting in touch with feelings.

The idea of confronting is to recognize honestly and directly and to point out to helpees what is going on or what you infer is going on. The effects are challenge, exposure, or threat. Resulting emotional effects are sometimes anxiety when challenged with feedback from the helper, and sometimes pleasure with his or her honest opinions and expressions of caring. In other words, confronting skills involve risk—resulting either in unwanted resistance from helpees or in desired openness of communication. It is a "telling it like it is" method that may threaten or thrill, depending on the timing and readiness of the helpee to be confronted with feedback honestly offered. We will look at the subskills of the confronting skill cluster in more detail below.

Recognizing Feeling

It is very apparent that one's ability to recognize and respond to feelings in helpees is based on the ability to recognize feelings in one's self. What do tenseness, sweating palms, twitching muscles, and fluttering eyelids say about one's own anxiety, guilt, anger, pleasure, or pain? Helpers must be aware of fine shades of feelings in themselves, which frequently are reactions to what the helpee is saying and can serve as guides to responses. For example, if helpers experience annoyance at what their helpees are saying, they must decide whether the goals of the relationship would be enhanced or retarded by expressing those feelings. As indicated in earlier discussions of countertransference feelings, the helper must make two judgments: Does this annoyance indicate problems I have as a person, or is it a reasonable reaction to what the helpee is saying? Depending on their theories of what is helpful, helpers usually *express* feelings they are aware of experiencing since their helpees sense them anyway from cues such as frowns and agitation.

Describing and Sharing Feeling

Sharing personal feelings about the helpee is a more intense form of self-disclosure than clarification responses. The principal value in describing feelings in one's self as a helper is that such a description helps to clarify how the helper feels. It also serves as a *model* for helpees to recognize and express their feelings. Helpees frequently do not understand the idea of expressing feeling, especially to near strangers—as helpers often appear to them initially. The condition of *trust* is dependent on an open sharing of feelings. Again, helpers can accelerate the process of building trust by sharing their own feelings. This "sharing of experience" as described in Brammer and Shostrom (1977) is one of the best ways to model the idea of "being a person." Some examples are the helper saying, "Your continuing on and on like that is boring me and I find myself getting sleepy." "I feel angry when you talk so much about wanting to hurt other people and not giving a damn about them." "It makes me feel good when you talk about yourself that way." You can see that this kind of response could have a reinforcing effect on helpees, because they are getting some rewards in the form of helper response for expressing feelings even when that response has a critical tone.

The *values for helpees* of sharing feelings are considerable. They experience relief from tensions (sometimes called emotional catharsis), satisfaction that they had the courage to face the feelings, and release of new creative energies.

The *limitations* of free expression of feelings by helpees (often called ventilation) are that they feel so good afterward that they consider it unnecessary to go on actively solving their problems. Sometimes, as we will see in the next chapter, expression of feeling is a goal in itself to provide relief from suffering. Most helpees have protective mechanisms for preventing them from revealing more feeling than they are able to tolerate, but helpers should be alert to occasions when helpee defenses are overwhelmed, and where their behaviors deteriorate under prolonged emotional catharsis. Helpers offering their services need colleagues, or specialist referral resources, to call on in such emergencies.

Some guidelines for knowing how far to let helpees ventilate and some cautions to observe follow. Be cautious about free expression of feeling if:

1. they are known to have severe emotional disorders—hysterical tendencies, delusional thinking, extreme anger, for example;
2. their lives are fraught with crises and emotionally demanding pressures such that discussing them mobilizes more feeling than they can handle;
3. their past history in dealing with emotional crises is known to be shaky;
4. strong resistance to exploration of feelings is noted;
5. adequacy of your own experience as a helper of disturbed people is doubtful;
6. your own emotional life is in turmoil;
7. time available for working through the feelings all the way is not adequate;
8. specialist support services are not available or adequate;
9. policies of your agency for exploring intense emotional life of clients is discouraged;
10. attitudes and expectations of parents or guardians of young helpees are not explored.

These guidelines are included to enhance your awareness of possible hazards in free expression of feeling, not to discourage you nor make you fearful about dealing with helpee feelings; they are included also because of the common idea in helping circles that sharing strong feelings always has desirable outcomes. If you find that sharing your own feelings, or working with helpees who are sharing their feelings, is uncomfortable or interferes with your effectiveness, it is a signal to do more work on your own feelings through means described in chapter 2.

An issue more common than excessive sharing of feelings is the helpee's underexpression or ignoring of his feelings. This condition is manifested when the helper focuses on *content* or when the helpee uses the phrase "I feel" when referring to an idea. Thus, helpees are unaware that they are avoiding feelings. An example is, "I feel that the best thing to do is not to go to college at this time." Depending on the tone, this statement expresses an opinion or a conclusion rather than a feeling. A feeling statement would be more like, "I'm afraid of going to college now. High school was such a bore." The principal goal of the helper in using the confronting skill is to challenge helpees to include honest feelings in their statements. One of the keys to this condition is to model expression of feeling yourself.

A confrontive way to get helpees to express feelings is to ask them to do so. Some examples are: "What are you feeling right now?" "You've described some facts about your situation; how do you feel about it?" "You have been saying what you think about your job, but I haven't sensed your true feelings about it yet. How do you feel about it?"

In summary, guidelines for describing and sharing feelings are:

1. *Share* your own feelings as a model.
2. *Ask* helpees to share their feelings.
3. Be *cautious* about the depth and extent of sharing.

Feedback and Opinion

Feedback is a term borrowed from electronics and physics where information is fed back into a system so that corrections can be made. Examples are thermostats that use information about temperature to activate the furnace switch, or guidance systems in space vehicles that feed information into the navigation equipment to correct the astronauts' course. Similarly, we give information in the form of opinions and reactions to helpees. As a result, they have a better idea of how they are performing, and they can use the information, if they so wish, to change their behavior.

One of the most valuable confrontive skills for developing understanding is honest feedback to helpees on how they affect you. We acquire our definitions of who we are by the reactions of other people to us. Our personalities are the total of our parents' opinions, chidings, and praises. Our helping relationships merely continue this basic process in a more focused fashion. Effective feedback from people they trust and know to care deeply about them can assist helpees to fill in gaps in their self-awareness.

The main *guidelines* for giving feedback are:

1. Give opinions in the form of feedback only when helpees are *ready*. This means that in most cases they will ask for feedback, but if not, the helper will ask if they would like some reactions. An example is, "We have been talking about your plans for the future; while you were listing your limitations I had some reactions." (Helpee's interest is aroused and the usual response is, "Oh? Tell me.") "Well, I'm con-

vinced from what you have told me about yourself that you are vastly underestimating your capabilities here; from my observations I think you express yourself very clearly and concisely, for example."

Feedback may be in the form of critical commentary, also, as in the following illustration: "We have been talking about your problems in getting along with people. You may be interested to know that I have been feeling increasingly irritated with your persistent quibbling about almost everything I say. I feel that I don't want to listen to you anymore. Do you think my reaction is typical of those of other people you know?"

Giving opinions without helpee readiness to make use of them is only likely to arouse resistance, resentment toward the helper, or outright denial since it would not fit the helpee's current self-opinion.

2. *Describe the behavior* before giving your reaction to it. Note in the illustrations above that the helper described the specific instance and then gave his or her feeling about it. This description keeps the responsibility for opinions on yourself. Often it is difficult to determine when the feedback is a projection of your personal prejudices and problems and when it is the kind of reaction that the helpee would get from most people. Feedback must be given cautiously, and with the clear understanding that the helper is offering his or her *personal* reactions to the helpee's behavior. Keeping reactions descriptive rather than evaluative leaves helpees free to use them as they see fit.

3. Give feedback in the form of *opinions about the behavior* rather than judgments about the person. It may seem like quibbling to separate the behavior from the person, but it is vastly different to say, "I don't like the way you constantly interrupt me," from "I don't like you because you are constantly interrupting me."

4. Give feedback about things that helpees have the *capacity to change.* It is not helpful to give feedback about physical characteristics or life circumstances, for example, which they would find very difficult to change.

5. Feedback should be *given in small amounts* so that helpees can experience the full impact of the helper's reaction. Too many items may overload them and create confusion and possible resentment. An example of such an overload would be, "I didn't like the way you spoke to me; I felt put down. Besides, you have been late consistently to our staff meetings and your progress reports have been getting skimpier, which has been irritating me even more." Feedback given in this cumulative manner serves more as ventilation of hostility for the giver, and less as a helpful gesture to the helpee.

6. Feedback should be a *prompt response* to current and specific behavior, not unfinished emotional business from the past. Being told,

for example, that one is "too forceful" is not as helpful as saying, "Just as we were about to decide what to do, you pushed your idea and seemed not to hear the other suggestions. I was conflicted about whether to resist you or just give in."

7. Ask the helpee for *reactions* to your feedback. Was it helpful or not? Did it enhance the relationship or diminish it?

Meditating

Meditating is a form of self-confrontation with ancient origins. Many philosophical groups in the Orient such as Zen, Yoga, and Sufi, along with the Christian and Hebrew traditions of the West, emphasize the values of self-understanding inherent in meditational forms. The main feature and principal value of meditation for the helping process is that it stops the active flow of ideas and actions and allows helpees to get in touch with themselves. Meditation opens the possibilities of awareness of self in relation to the world, which is a different process from the usual rational sensory types of awareness. Our Western languages have few forms in which to express these nonrational or esoteric experiences. Zen, for example, emphasizes awareness through a state of "no mind" where the flow of consciousness stops. Various styles of meditation are aided by special postures, mantras (repeated vocalizations), contemplating an object, or breathing exercises, but the basic idea of stopping action and thought to allow other forms of experience is the same among them.

If you decide that this meditational form of self-confrontation would be useful to your helpees, you should become familiar with at least one of the styles mentioned above and experience it first yourself. A few general principles can help, even if you are relatively unsophisticated about specific meditational forms. Helpees who flit from topic to topic and who have difficulty getting in touch with their feelings, for example, might be helped through some kind of meditation. You can ask your helpees to stop talking, close their eyes, get in a comfortable position, and just be quiet awhile. You might ask them to focus on their breathing—how they inhale and exhale and to let the ideas flitting across their awareness just fade away.

The value for helpees of this method is that it should open new doors to their feelings and awareness of themselves in relation to others and their physical environment. If nothing else, it should help them to calm down and should prepare them for a new approach to their problems. To obtain maximum value from meditational methods, helpees should practice them in everyday life also.

Here is a summary of guidelines for using meditational forms of self-confrontation:

1. Be familiar with one or more styles through *personal experience.*
2. *Explain* the value of the method to the helpees.
3. Ask them to assume a relaxed *comfortable position* with eyes closed.
4. Ask them to be *quiet* and to let their thoughts fade away.
5. Ask them to focus on their *breathing* as a means of getting in touch with their body processes and feelings.
6. After a few minutes ask them to open their eyes and *describe the experience* using leads from feeling statements to encourage further exploration.
7. Ask them to *practice* this confrontational form at home if they find it productive and satisfying.

Repeating

Repeating is another method of self-confrontation, prompted by the helper, which comes out of the gestalt tradition. The helpee is asked merely to repeat a word, phrase, or short sentence one or more times. The helper suggests that helpees focus on one of their statements that appear to have intense meaning for them. The helper then asks them to repeat it in simple direct form. The purpose is to generate more feelings associated with those words as the repetitions continue. The helper asks them to try to hear what they are saying emotionally with the repetitions. Then either they discuss the feelings precipitated or the feeling spills out in a form such as tears.

The value for helpees of this kind of confronting is that they can tap feelings that are obscured behind long sentences and constant topic changes. It breaks up their usual method of discourse suddenly, which generally serves to provoke intense feelings. The simplicity of the repetition method evokes little resistance from helpees. It puts them into a simple childlike frame of thinking that cuts through their sophisticated adult verbiage. Finally, it offers to the helpee a means of focusing on significant feelings and of avoiding the temptation to move quickly on to safer topics.

The judgment involved is knowing when to ask helpees to repeat and how often to prompt them with requests such as "Say it again," or "Again . . . again." This process is continued until the feeling comes out in verbal or nonverbal form such as crying or striking. The same process can be used with gestures. If you see a helpee shaking his fist, for example, you might ask him to "Do that again." It focuses his attention on the emotional impact of the gesture. An example of the repeating method of self-confrontation is:

He: I don't have any friends; people don't love me, I guess.

Hr: Say that again, "People don't love me."

He: People don't love me. People don't love me. (Pause) Maybe I'm not very lovable.

Hr: Say again, "I'm not lovable."

He: I'm not lovable.

Hr: Again.

He: I'm not lovable.

This kind of repeating opens the possibilities for significant confrontation of self-regarding attitudes that are hindering effective personal and interpersonal functioning. It brings painful feelings to the point where they can be discussed directly.

Guidelines for the repeating method are:

1. Note *statements* or *gestures* with feeling implications.
2. Ask the helpee to *repeat* the key word, phrase, or short sentence one or more times until feelings are evoked.
3. *Encourage* the helpee to keep the repetition in the present active verb tense.
4. Allow sufficient *time* for the emotional impact to be felt and sorted out meaningfully by the helpee before going on to another topic.

Associating

Associating is another skill to facilitate the loosening of feelings. It is a more precise form of the old "free association" method where helpees were encouraged to say whatever crossed their awareness. The goal was to get helpees loosened from their precise, logical, planned statements and into the more fragmentary and illogical realm of feelings. You suggest, for example, "Tell me what is on your mind, and say it even if it seems vague and unimportant." "Let yourself go." "Just give me pieces of ideas; don't try to be logical."

Another variation of associating method is to pick out a word from helpees' statements that seems to have emotional significance for them.

You then ask them to give all the other words that come to awareness in rapid order, and you note them for discussion later. An example is:

Hr: You seem to be fixed on your mother's influence on you. I suggest that you say the word "mother" and follow it with as many words as you can think of in rapid order. Do you understand?

He: Yes, I think so. Mother—love, soft, fun, spank . . .

The main outcome expected for helpees is a freeing of feelings so they are more available for direct discussion. It also gets to feelings faster than usual discussion methods.

In summary, guidelines for association skills are:

1. Ask helpees to *say what comes* to their awareness.
2. *Explain* that the flowing ideas do not need to be logical or consistent.
3. *Use the results* to aid helpees into further exploration of feelings or discussion of the results of their associating.
4. As a variation, *pick out a word* with possible emotional significance from helpee statements and ask them to say freely all the thoughts and feelings evoked by that word as fast as they come.

Skill Cluster 6: Interpreting

Interpreting is an active helper process of explaining the meaning of events to helpees so that they are able to see their problems in new ways. The main goal is to teach helpees to interpret events in their lives by themselves. In *paraphrasing,* the helpee's internal frame of reference is maintained, whereas through *interpretation* the helper offers a new frame of reference. Interpretation is used more in formal psychotherapy than in similar styles of helping because of therapists' needs to think diagnostically. They must be formulating hunches all the time about what is going on and what might be a logical explanation for their helpees' behaviors. They do not always share these thoughts, since they serve primarily to help them understand what is going on in their helpees. Many helpers feel this kind of thinking hinders the helping process because the helper becomes preoccupied with thinking *about* or *ahead* of helpees rather than *with* them. This shift to an external frame of reference in the helper is one of the main limitations of using interpretive skills.

Interpretations often are given in terms of some special theory of personality change held by the helper. Usually these explanations are expressed as hypotheses, or hunches, about what is happening. The best method of becoming familiar with the many styles of interpreting is to watch films or listen to tapes of different helpers.

Interpreting is similar to reflecting, but interpreting adds the helper's meanings to the helpee's basic message. When you decide that an interpretation might be helpful, look for the basic message of the helpee (as in reflecting and paraphrasing), restate it in capsule form, then add your understanding of what the helpee has said (the interpreting). If the interpretation makes sense to the helpee it will accelerate the interview. If the interpretation is not meaningful, try again. You must also be confident that your interpretation was essentially accurate, since it may take some time before its significance to the helpee sinks in. Interpreting means that you are leading helpees to seek wider understandings of their feelings and broader perceptions. You must recognize that occasionally you will be too far removed from the helpee, and then you will need to aim a little closer to the helpee's level of awareness. It should be understood clearly that the *goal* of all interpretive effort is *self-interpretation* by the helpee and increasing the helpee's ability to act effectively.

Some examples of interpretation at a simple level without an elaborate theoretical rationale are: "You have told me about your family as if you were a disinterested observer. I gather you have no specific feeling about them." "It is possible for people to both love and hate their fathers at the same time." "Perhaps you can see that your feelings of hostility toward men might be at the root of your marital difficulties."

Interpretive Questions

Some interpreting is done in the form of questions such as, "Do you think then that you distrust men because your father treated you so badly?" This questioning form implies a more tentative quality than the declarative statements and makes interpreting less risky for the helper. Interpretive questions have focusing effect also, such as in the following illustration where the helpee has been avoiding discussion of his self-concerns.

Hr: When are you going to be concerned about yourself too?
He: That is a selfish attitude.
Hr: So, what's wrong with that?
He: I don't like selfish people.

Hr: Because . . .?

He: Selfish people aren't very popular.

Hr: So, popularity is important to you; and if you are too self-centered, people won't like you. Is that getting close to where you are?

Fantasy and Metaphor Interpretations

Another stylized way of introducing an interpretation is to put it in the form of a fantasy (daydream), even using the picture language of a metaphor. An example is, "I have a fantasy about what you have just said. I picture you walking down a path in the woods, coming to a fork in the path, and being undecided which one to choose. You unconcernedly flip a coin and run joyfully down the path chosen by the coin. How does this fit?" If the fantasy is close to the helpees' awareness, it will trigger new ways of perceiving themselves. The limitation is that in using this skill helpers shift into their own frame of reference, thus forcing helpees to deal with them (or their fantasies). Sometimes it is useful just to give one's reaction in the form of a metaphor, such as, "Most of the time I perceive you as a great big soft teddy bear who stays in any position he is placed."

I have mentioned the idea of *levels* of interpreting several times. Interpreting could be placed on a continuum from reflecting, where you stay at the meaning and feeling level of the helpee, through elaborate theoretical explanation of behavior in depth interpretation. Even in so-called depth interpretation we do not dig deeply into the helpees' psyches and come up with brilliant insights that unfold the mysteries of their personalities. This is a popular view that came from distorted perceptions of psychoanalytic methods.

The following illustration offers a few of these ways of responding at different levels of meaning. The helpee says, "I was at a party last night where I drank too much. I broke into tears and cried and cried. I acted like a child who wanted to go home to mother. I feel so ashamed." Your response, at different levels, might be one of the following:

1. You drank to the point where tears came freely. You're ashamed now as you talk about it. (content paraphrase)
2. You feel very badly about what happened last night. (general feeling reflection)
3. You feel badly that you lost control of yourself last night. (mild interpreting—adding the idea of control)

4. You drank until you lost control of your feelings. As you look back on the evening now you want to punish yourself for acting that childish way. (interpreting—adding idea of punishing and reverting to childhood patterns)

5. Your drinking, crying, and mentioning mother, makes me wonder if you want to go back to mother—like being dependent on her for comfort and feeling you can't stand on your own two feet. (deeper level interpreting—desire for a comforting mother and dependency)

6. (Interpreting his statement according to some theoretical framework, like gestalt, which might explain in terms of giving up dependency on others and substituting self-dependency; or the rational-emotive approach for getting rid of self-defeating and self-punishing feelings about one's behavior; or psychoanalytic interpretations about wishes to go back to the womb. Behaviorally oriented helpers might inquire about the helpees' desires to change their drinking or crying behavior.)

The topic of the myriad verbal forms for couching interpreting skills is really too complex to cover in detail in this basic helping skills book, but it would be wrong to understate the significance and usefulness of interpreting skill for the average helper. We should know not only the possible uses, but also the implications for misuse. Further readings in the references at the end of this chapter will add to your understanding of various styles of interpretation.

The main consequences for helpees of being confronted through interpretation are broadened perceptions of meanings of their behaviors and different ways of viewing their problems and possible solutions. Generally speaking, helpees can expect a deeper understanding of their problems as a result of the added perspectives of the helper. If you get the "Suddenly I realized" reaction, you know your interpreting has been successful. Interpreting also has the effect of intensifying the emotional involvement of helpees so that they will take more responsibility for their own interpreting.

Guidelines for interpreting are:

1. Look for the *basic message(s)* of the helpees.
2. *Paraphrase* these to them.
3. Add *your understanding* of what their messages mean in terms of your theory or your general explanation of motives, defenses, needs, styles.
4. Keep the *language simple* and the *level close to their messages.* Avoid wild speculation and statements in esoteric words.

5. *Introduce* your ideas with statements that indicate you are offering *tentative ideas* on what their words or behaviors mean. Examples are: "Is this a fair statement" "The way I see it is" "I wonder if" or "Try this one on for size."
6. Solicit *helpee reactions* to your interpretations.
7. *Teach helpees* to do their own interpreting. Remember, we can't give insight to others; they must make their own discoveries.

Skill Cluster 7: Informing

This skill of information giving is so commonplace that it needs no elaboration. It is included here to indicate that sharing simple facts possessed by helpers is sometimes the most helpful thing they could do. Some kinds of information in the expertise category, such as information from test instruments, require special skills for planning and decision making that are beyond the scope of this general helping book. Further information on skills for informing about interests, aptitudes, and personality traits may be obtained from Brammer and Shostrom (1977) and the suggested readings section at the end of this chapter.

Another category of information about services concerning financial planning, career planning, and family planning needs to be handled by specially informed people through referral skills to be described in the next chapter.

Advice

Advice giving is a common type of informing activity by helpers. Helpees, expecting some kind of expert pronouncements in the form of sound advice on what to do, often thrust the helper into the role of expert. Beginning helpers, too, often perceive their function as giving "common sense" advice. Before reading further I suggest you formulate your own ideas about giving and receiving advice. How do you feel when people advise you? Under what conditions in your life has advice been helpful? What were the characteristics of the adviser? Do age or experience make any difference? Conversely, how do you feel about giving advice? Are there differences between giving advice and offering information?

There is a long tradition of giving advice in the helping folklore. It is a common occurrence between persons who know and trust one another. This time-honored function among friends is often beneficial. Issues arise, however, when helpees consult helpers in their larger environments at work, church, or school. These institutions have many natural self-styled advice givers who often have attractive charismatic qualities. As a consequence, they are sought out by confused and troubled people, largely because they are attractive people with a reputation for being helpful. These persons could just as well be janitors or clerks as well as those with helping titles such as ministers or teachers. Helpees without serious emotional disabilities often do not want psychotherapy or counseling, but seek advice mainly on a particular problem. What they often search for is an empathic listener who will not attempt to "psych them out," "play the therapy game," or become a psychological version of "wet nurse."

In an informal study of what Korner* called "indigenous counselors" he found that almost all bureaucratic organizations had such an informally appointed advice giver in the small group structures. This person's function, according to Korner's data, is to become the organization's human behavior lay-expert. His data from people who consulted these indigenous advisers indicate that such advisers enjoy talking to people, appreciate the respect and confidence people place in them, appear self-confident and dignified, and are very willing to give of their store of accumulated problem-solving experience in a no-nonsense neutral manner. They had an unusual quality to get to the core of the matter and inspire confidence and trust. The advice was offered in a manner that did not obligate the receiver to follow it or seek subsequent meetings for further help. Receivers were careful to indicate that this adviser did not offer solace and support to reduce psychic discomfort. The main contributions of the indigenous advice givers were to crystallize and focus issues, to clarify decision processes, and to move beyond the impasse. It appears that persons perceived as helpful advice givers use helping skills far beyond sheer conventional advice. These findings suggest also that such indigenous helpers in organizations are performing useful services to people informally and could probably enhance their effectiveness with additional work on helping skills. Unfortunately, Korner's data did not reveal the nature or the consequences of "bad advice."

Giving advice in the traditional manner is a controversial topic in helping literature. Some writers claim advising reflects the arrogance of helpers who assume they are so all-knowing that they can advise other persons on a course of action. Critics also claim advice is ineffective and fosters dependency. Yet others assert that advice giving is helpful under some circumstances. Advice can be helpful if it is given by trusted persons with expert opinions based on solid knowledge of a supporting field such as law, medicine, or child rearing. Sometimes

*Korner, I. Unpublished paper "About Advice Giving."

helpees need a recommended course of action supported by wide experience, and it is hoped, by facts. There is a place for suggestions that leave the evaluation and the final decision about courses of action completely open to the helpee. You can suggest hypotheses that need checking before acting and ways of approaching problems. Examples are situations in which parents are exploring ways of handling rebellious children, or students are weighing choices about courses. The use of considered suggestions is appropriate when the contact is short and the decision relatively inconsequential in the person's life.

Advice is often appropriate in crisis situations where several people must cooperate to prepare helpees for major readjustments of their life circumstances, such as family reorganization after hospitalization, divorce, imprisonment, unemployment, or financial loss. Advice is wholly inappropriate for dealing with major individual choice questions, such as, "Should I get a divorce?" or "What career should I enter?"

Most people object to advice given in the form of "father knows best," or offhand suggestions tempered with strong persuasion. Usually, persons giving the advice have a strong stake in the helpee's following advice, and their persuasive attitude often generates hostility in helpees.

The principal limitation of advice giving is that helpees usually don't follow it. They often seemingly ask, or even beg, for advice but they are most often asking themselves the rhetorical question, "What shall I do?" They may be expressing dependent feelings, knowing full well what to do. If helpers fall into this trap they justifiably incur the wrath or contempt of the helpee. A more productive strategy, especially if there is time, is to deal with the feelings involved first. The main task is to distinguish between the honest and direct request for information or suggestions and the expression of indecisive or dependent feelings. When in doubt, it is more productive to try a reflecting approach with the presumed feelings first, and then deal with the request itself.

Some other limitations of giving advice are that they reinforce dependence on experts, which shifts responsibility to the helper for solutions. Frequently, helpers who take the "If I were you" approach are projecting their own needs, problems, or values into the advice rather than keeping the helpee's needs foremost. Experience in group forms of helping indicates that often participants begin giving advice because they unconsciously perceive the other person's problems as their own; therefore, they are really speaking to themselves. Another limitation, furthermore, is that the helpee may take the helper's advice and later find that it was invalid. The helper then is blamed when things don't turn out right in the helpee's life.

A summary of guidelines for informing skills is as follows:

1. Be *informed,* or know the sources of information, in your area of advertised expertise.
2. Do not use educational or psychological test instruments without thorough *training* in their uses and limitations.
3. Don't use advice unless it is in the form of *tentative suggestions* based on solid expertise.

Expected Outcomes

After reading this chapter you should be able to: (1) list the seven main clusters of skills for promoting awareness of understanding self and environment; (2) cite subskills in the clusters and illustrate their uses and misuses with examples from helping interviews; (3) apply the skills, after practice and feedback from associates, according to strategies suggested in chapter 7.

Suggestions for Further Study

Amos, W., and Grambs, J., *Counseling the Disadvantaged Youth.* Englewood Cliffs, N.J.: Prentice-Hall, 1968. (Special skills needed to work with helpees from disadvantaged groups.)

Benjamin, A., *The Helping Interview.* Boston: Houghton Mifflin, 1969. (Ch. 5 on the use of questions, and ch. 7 on leading and reflecting.)

Brammer, L., and Shostrom, E., *Therapeutic Psychology: Fundamentals of Actualization Counseling and Psychotherapy.* 3rd ed. Englewood Cliffs, N.J.: Prentice-Hall, 1977. (Ch. 7 on relationship techniques, ch. 9 on interpretation techniques, ch. 10 on advice, information, and tests.)

Evans, D., Hearn, M., Uhlemann, M., and Ivey, A., *Essential Interviewing.* Monterey, Ca.: Brooks/Cole, 1978. (A programed text offering students the opportunity to practice microskills in the context of the ongoing interview.)

Gordon, T., *Parent Effectiveness Training.* New York: Peter H. Wyden, 1970. (Chs. 3–7 on listening methods with children.)

Levy, L., *Psychological Interpretation.* New York: Holt, Rinehart & Winston, 1963. (A detailed presentation of interpretive techniques.)

Ligon, M., and McDaniel, S., *The Teacher's Role in Counseling.* Englewood Cliffs, N.J.: Prentice-Hall, 1970. (Ch. 5 on the gathering and use of information.)

Perez, J., *The Initial Counseling Contact.* Boston: Houghton Mifflin, 1968. (Ch. 4, practical techniques in the initial contact, Appendix A, sample of a verbatim first interview.)

ROGERS, C., *Client-Centered Therapy*. Boston: Houghton Mifflin, 1951. (Description, rationale, and illustrations of reflecting skills.)

SUPER, D., and CRITES, J., *Appraising Vocational Fitness by Means of Psychological Testing*. New York: Harper & Row, 1962. (An overview and depth study of the tests used in vocational counseling.)

FIVE

Helping Skills for Comfort and Crisis Utilization

One of the most common helping functions is providing relief from psychological suffering. Social service literature contains many practical ideas for dealing with specific types of situational crises, and traditional religions have had much to say about human suffering, hope, and existential crises. But according to Darbonne (1967), who surveyed and summarized the scanty crisis literature spanning twenty years, there has been little systematic information for the general helper. Only in the past decade have helping professionals become interested in "crisis intervention" (Aguilera and Messick 1974). This chapter summarizes ideas about crises and skills for the general helper who gives support during loss and stress.

In general, dealing with people in crisis calls for flexibility of response, rapid and active intervening, and setting limited goals for getting the person as functional as possible in a limited time. Although there are some special skills available for providing comfort and managing crises, the personhood, or "self as instrument," of helpers is a more important consideration. Their values, life styles, and personality traits have a profound impact on helpees' ability to face stress and crises. Thus, helpers cannot depend only on their bank of skills and strategies, but must draw on a variety of sources—including religion, philosophy, behavioral science, and the helping professions—for their values, ideas, and skills. Behavioral scientists alone, though they produce most of the concepts and methods for testing helper effectiveness, cannot offer belief systems, values to live by, or hope to suffering persons. Many of the skills described in the previous chapter can also be applied in crises, since they provide support functions and promote understanding.

This chapter will: (1) describe outcomes you may expect from reading this chapter; (2) define and discuss terms used in crisis work; (3) describe strategies for helping people in crisis; (4) describe skills to facilitate support in times of stress and crisis; and (5) list suggestions for further reading.

Before delving into strategies and methods developed by helping specialists I recommend that you stop to think over events in your own life where you experienced suffering and perhaps a crisis—bereavement, illness, umemployment, or severe stress. What sources of help were available and which did you seek? What strategies or methods were helpful to you in working through your crisis? What comforting characteristics did the helper exhibit? Which were most useful among your self-help approaches? To what extent did you include writings from religion, philosophy, and the behavioral sciences? How helpful were these self-directed readings?

Outcomes You Can Expect

From studying this chapter you will be competent to: (1) identify skills and strategies useful in situations requiring support and comfort; (2) identify understanding skills that also have a supportive function; (3) use the terminology for describing crisis and stress; and (4) exercise judgment on strategies to be used in stress and crisis situations. The ultimate degree of your effectiveness will be measured by helpees' improved ability to cope with crises, and by their demonstrated ability to translate crises into growth opportunities.

Human Conditions of Concern

It is difficult to classify human problems meaningfully and to separate cause and effect. Stress and crisis conditions can be divided into three categories: loss due to outside factors, internal distress regardless of cause, and transitional states that demand adaptive responses. Some illustrative conditions are:

Loss

Bereavement	Divorce
Unemployment	Imprisonment
Disaster	

Internal Distress

Hopelessness	Battle fatigue
Despair	Bad drug trips
Depression	Suicide attempts

Transitional States

Job change	Family conflict
Relocation	Impending threat
New family member	Illness

Hill (1958) classified stress in family crises into external and internal factors. A stress-producing crisis that originates *outside* the family, such as war, persecution, or natural disaster often solidifies family efforts to resolve the stress. *Internal* family crises, however, such as suicide, nonsupport, infidelity, or alcoholism often result in disintegrating family ties because these behaviors reflect on the competence of the family to cope with its own affairs. Hill further classifies crises on the basis of effect on the family. Examples are: (1) dismemberment (loss of family member); (2) accession (surprise addition of member); and (3) demoralization (decreased morale). These conditions eventually result in a major family crisis, preceded usually by progressive disintegration. Figure 6 illustrates the wide range of problems that can precipitate family crises.

Definition of Terms

Stress

Stress is a condition characterized by physiological tension and persistent choice conflict. The helpee feels under pressure to reduce the tension and achieve comfort or equilibrium. Often the resolution takes a maladaptive form, such as illness, without awareness in the helpee.

FIGURE 6. A CLASSIFICATION OF FAMILY CRISES OF DISMEMBERMENT—ACCESSION AND DEMORALIZATION (REPRODUCED FROM HILL, 1958, p. 38.)

Dismemberment Only

Death of child, spouse, or parent
Hospitalization of spouse
War separation

Accession Only

Unwanted pregnancy
Deserter returns
Stepfather, stepmother additions
Some war reunions
Some adoptions, aged grandparents, orphaned kin

Demoralization Only

Nonsupport
Infidelity
Alcoholism
Drug addiction
Delinquency and events bringing disgrace

Demoralization Plus Dismemberment or Accession

Illegitimacy
Runaways
Desertion
Divorce
Imprisonment
Suicide or homicide
Institutionalization for mental illness

Stress is a more pervasive and less intense condition than crisis; but it may continue for unlimited time, with or without the provoking stimulus.

Stress is cumulative, and though individual events appear to have little impact, the cumulation over a year can contribute to major crises, such as illness. Holmes and Rahe (1967), who studied the effects of such cumulative stress events in relation to health, found that a person with a high cumulative point index, based on events scaled in intensity from death to parking tickets, was likely to suffer a major health problem that year.

Clients must be helped to an awareness of the nature and power of stressors in their lives as well as the buildup of minor stress to crisis proportions. Helpees need to realize that the transitional states between periods of relative stability—school to work, marriage to singlehood—are normal conditions that require specific self-help skills and, sometimes, helper support to cope with.

Crisis

Crisis is a state of disorganization in which helpees face frustration of important life goals or profound disruption of their life cycles and methods of coping with stress. The term *crisis* refers usually to the helpee's feelings about the disruption, not the disruption itself. Crises are limited in time, usually lasting not more than a few weeks.

There are normal *developmental* crises, such as birth or a child going off to school. *Situational* crises are associated with severe loss of status, possessions, or loved ones. *Existential* crises refer to the conflicts and anxious feelings experienced when facing the significant human issues of purpose, responsibility, freedom, and commitment. Although this type of crisis is a normal part of human existence it becomes a true crisis when one becomes aware of old forms of constricted being and new possibilities for action. For some, these pressures to choose and to act assume crisis proportions. If they are not resolved in a constructive way through normal living or special helping processes, the crisis eventuates in feelings that range from detached boredom and purposelessness, to despair over forced responsibility for choice, and finally to panic and disintegration.

Four *phases* of a crisis period have been described by Caplan (1964). An adaptation of his phases follows: (1) Initial tension is experienced, which arouses habitual adaptive responses. (2) Tension increases under continuous stimulation, and lack of success is experienced in coping and tension reduction. This frustration is complicated by distress and inefficiency. (3) Tension increases until emergency resources, internal and external, are mobilized. The crisis may be eased temporarily through such emergency coping mechanisms, seeing the problem differently, or relinquishing goals. (4) An acute phase follows if the crisis is not eased in stage 3, or averted by denial or resignation. Tension mounts to the point where major dysfunctions in behavior develop, and/or emotional control is lost.

Although a crisis state may precipitate either complete dysfunction or no observable response, it may also create the seeds of considerable growth. The helpee can be highly influenced at this stage. The *values* of crisis can be realized if the person is now ready to reach for higher levels of self-realization, as well as calm equilibrium. Availability of the helping process is thus crucial at this early stage because the helpee is so malleable and ready for change. Parad (1965) cites many instances where agencies practicing crisis intervention have productive outcomes when help is offered and accepted early.

In addition to the availability of helping relationships, the psychological background and makeup of the person determine to a great extent his or her reaction to prolonged stress and intensive crises. We cannot assume when disaster strikes or when a family seems to be going through enormous stress that some kind of massive help is necessary. Some persons and families have enormous reserves to draw on.

Through scrutiny of short case histories, Bloom (1963) studied the problem of how helping professionals viewed crises. These histories contained varying amounts of five elements usually constituting a crisis condition: (1) awareness of the precipitating event; (2) rapidity of onset; (3) presence of discomfort; (4) external evidence of behavior disruption; and (5) rapidity of resolution. Bloom found that helpers defined a crisis largely in terms of precipitating events and to some extent time of resolution, but a problem arose when trying to differentiate between those profound events that led to a crisis state and those that did not. This lack of precision in defining a crisis makes it very difficult to determine the effectiveness of a particular strategy or method.

Support

Support is a condition in which the helpee feels secure and comfortable psychologically. It includes awareness of well-being and satisfaction of "affect hunger." Support comes from three sources: (1) the relationship itself where the helpee experiences the helper's acceptance and warmth; (2) experiencing direct help in the form of reassurance or environmental support; (3) experiencing the helper's assumption of major responsibility in the relationship as a temporary expedient to reduce stress. Whether to encourage support actively is controversial among helpers. Some helpers claim that providing support is a necessary helping function, especially for persons in states of crisis. Helpees need comfort and security to recoup their coping forces, and the interview definitely should not add to this stress. Others assert that deliberately providing support reduces an opportunity for growth. They claim that helpees should take advantage of the "shaken up" condition to explore new avenues of growth, take new risks, complete their "grief work," and make new plans, if the crisis involves bereavement. The psychological "first aid" should be the supportive quality of the helper's attentive and caring presence only.

One *value* of providing direct support is reduction of debilitating anxiety, and consequent psychological comfort. Helpees who feel inadequate, unworthy, grief stricken, lonely, or fearful are given a supportive helper during the peak of their crisis, or the depth of their feelings, until they can marshal their strength to go on. In such a supportive relationship helpees can feel that they do not need to be strong and capable for awhile; it is like feeling that they can "walk" before they need to "run." Support conditions allow them to express and face their dependency and security needs.

Grief-stricken persons in a supportive relationship also feel that they are not alone, that someone understands, and that they are free to share their hurts. Similarly, a supportive relationship helps persons fearful of their impulses to express strong feelings of despair and frustration without being hurt more. Proper support also assures helpees that they can help themselves, that they are capable, that they are worthy, or that they can plan. Feeling, for example, that they can save a marriage gives them the courage to keep trying for solutions.

Finally, a supportive relationship assures helpees that they do not need to take impulsive action that might increase their difficulties. They can take sufficient time to get their feelings sorted out and to explore alternatives before acting. An example is introducing "stop time" before initiating a divorce proceeding.

Some of the *limitations* of supportive relationships were implied above. Briefly, a major limitation is the creation of dependence on the helper as a source of support. Sometimes helpees feel resentful, or even guilty, when they are recipients of support. Occasionally they experience dependence on the helper. Some are threatened by too much warmth and closeness because they have not yet learned how to manage a close human relationship when they are hurting.

Supportive efforts that come across as sympathy may be interpreted by helpees as insincere and gimmicky. Overuse of reassurance, for example, makes the helper sound shallow to the helpee. For example, helpees have often heard the platitudes that "everything will come out in the wash, so don't fret"; and "every cloud has a silver lining." They know from experience that it is not true that things always turn out "right" or for the "best," especially if you or someone else has just given them some bad news. If a man has received negative evaluations of his work performance, he usually knows he has been unsatisfactory. Nothing is gained from "sweetening" the news, or from assuring him that some "miracle" is going to happen or that people do not "understand" him. A strategy likely to produce much more growth would be to help him to evaluate the feedback about his work objectively and to accept the judgments to the extent of their validity.

Hope and Despair

These twin concepts merit extended discussion in this context of support and crisis utilization because they are so central to the helpee's recovery of his equilibrium, management of stress, and prevention of future crises. Korner (1970) has examined hope as a method of coping, a means of preventing crises, and as a route to healthy behavior. He points out that helpers appear to have mixed reactions about the values of hope. On the one hand, they believe that hope makes stress tolerable, but they are convinced also that it is foolhardy to rely on "false hopes," or to use hope to avoid acting responsibly in the present. Few studies have been made of the helping functions of hope, but the general opinion among professional helpers seems to be that the elusive quality of hope is more a wishful panacea than a dependable aid to solving personal problems.

Instead of defining hope as expectations in the absence of verifiable facts, it has been more fruitful to look at its opposite, hopelessness or despair. The anguish and pain of this condition are well known. Despair implies that people have given up, that they have stopped trying to change the cause, that they feel dejected, and that they accept the inevitability of the feared outcome. Korner indicates that "hope induces a feeling of 'assumed certainty' that the dreaded event will not happen, that despair will not occur" (1970, p. 135). He goes on to say that "hope is an assumption which is clung to because it is of fundamental importance to the life of the individual" (p. 136). When helpees become aware of these assumptions they may continue to use them as rationalizations to avoid despair, or they may see them as wishful thinking. In the latter case, they can manage them rationally in terms of their reality at that moment.

While hope remains primarily an emotional experience for helpees, they can think and talk about it also. Thus, hope involves expectancies that are different from simple wishes for events that might occur. The central characteristic of hope for helpees is a "quality of personal dependence on outcome" (Korner 1970, p. 135), without building their actions "on 'expectations' that it *must* happen in order to avoid undesirable and disagreeable dreaded outcomes" (Ibid., p. 135).

Some supportive *values of hoping* are momentary comfort and relief from suffering. Hope mobilizes reserved energy to meet present and future sources of stress. For some it means psychological, and even physical, survival. Medical folklore is full of instances where hope sustained, and apparently facilitated recovery of the "incurably" ill.

A *limitation* that the helper should watch for is the tendency for hope to become an escape from unpleasant realities or responsibilities. It is also easy for hopes to be transformed into more superficial, unrealistic wishes. The consequences of giving up wishes are not as great as losing hope. If the former happens, the helpee may be disappointed, but if hope diminishes, the person is vulnerable to doubt, or at worst, despair, insecurity, helplessness, and immobility.

Grief and Loss

Grief is a normal emotional reaction to severe loss, usually of a significant person. An acute grief reaction may come considerably after the loss or traumatic event, or it may not come at all in the manner expected. Grief feelings following bereavement may take a normal predictable course, called "grief work," or they may be expressed in distorted and dysfunctional behaviors. Lindemann (1944), who has written about acute grief most systematically, described the course of normal and morbid grief in a form useful for general helpers.

Normal grief is characterized by: (1) physical reactions—body distress in waves of twenty minutes to an hour, tightness and choking, sleeplessness, digestive disturbances, loss of appetite, sighing and shortness of breath, and weakness; (2) feelings of emptiness, tension, exhaustion, loss of warmth, and awareness of distance from people; (3) occasional preoccupation with images of the deceased; (4) occasional feelings of guilt over failure to do something, or exaggerations of self-accusations over small incidents; (5) change in activity patterns, restlessness, aimlessness, and searching for activity, yet lacking energy and motivation to follow through.

Morbid grief reactions are exaggerations of normal grief behaviors and may take the form of underreaction or delayed grief which may come years after the loss. Other forms are prolonged isolation, flights into expansiveness and well-being, unusually strong irritability or hostility toward friends and relatives, and prolonged depression. These reactions require specialized care, and the bereaved should be brought to the attention of a specialist, preferably a psychiatrist experienced in grief work, since medication is usually one of the supportive treatments utilized. All available human resources need to be involved, even more than in normal grief reactions. Depending on the specific individual's wishes and background, the involvement of ministers, with their traditional comforting rituals, reassurances, and relationships, could help persons accept and relieve their suffering.

Lindemann (1944) described the "anticipatory grief reaction" that complicates relationships when prolonged absence, such as wartime, is present. After the separation, grief reactions sometimes take place and are worked through as if the absent person had died. When the absentee returns, as in the case of military personnel, both parties often are surprised at the emotional detachment of their reunion. The grief work had been carried out so effectively, probably as a protection in case of a death notice, that the spouse at home had no remaining feeling for the absentee. Such situations call for a delicate rebuilding of relationships or facing the decision to remain separated.

The *normal course* of grief work consists of: (1) *accepting* the grief work process; (2) *expressing* the feelings of grief; (3) *dealing* with the memory of the deceased; (4) *readjusting* to the new environment without the deceased; (5) *building* new relationships. An important element in the helping process is to enable the bereaved to accept and work through this grief process.

Although this section has dealt with grief and loss in terms of bereavement and disaster, the principles apply to less intense reactions to loss, such as employment, property, or reputation. The strategies to follow are applicable to the full range of loss reactions from intense grief in bereavement to disappointment over a missed promotion. These strategies also apply to crises other than loss, such as conflict, arrest, and persecution.

Strategies for Helping in Crises

The discussions below suggest general strategies for helping persons under sustained stress or in a crisis. Simple formulas cannot ease human suffering, especially the sudden distress caused by uncontrolled traumatic events. Reactions to crises are highly individualistic and involve fundamental issues around the meaning of human existence. Even though it seems presumptuous to think of "helping" under such extreme conditions as life/death, some general helping principles apply to all types of crises. The first is liberal use of *emotional support* through close contact, reassurance, and listening to feelings. Often *changes in the environment,* such as taking the person to a safe and quiet place with nurturant and understanding people, are indicated.

Crisis Intervention Steps

A more specific series of four crisis intervention steps are required when the helper is in a more formal and responsible helping role. The helper first *appraises* (determines) the current condition of the person and the nature and severity of the crisis. An estimation must be made of the degree of risk or danger before emergency action is taken in a case such as a suicide threat, for example. The appraisal of the person's situation includes how much disruption the person is experiencing. To obtain perspective on the present crisis, the helper may need to delve into immediately preceding conditions.

The helper must then *decide on the type of help* most needed at the moment based on an appraisal of the adjustment skills of the person. What resources are available to the person (such as a support group or a friend), and what personal strengths are available to help restore the person to a minimum level of functioning?

The third step is to *act* in a directly helpful way. The helper assists the person to vent present feelings of fear, guilt, or anger. In addition, the helper helps the person to expand options for action, or at least to acquire an intellectual grasp of the plight. The helper assists people in crisis mobilize their defense mechanisms and adjusting skills. Through suggestions, the helper opens new possibilities for action and new relationships with people. These new options may include referral to a specialist for intensive counseling.

While working through the action steps the person begins to *resolve the state of crisis* and to achieve renewed equilibrium. Here the helper reinforces the adaptive skills the person has mobilized to reduce the tension and formulates a plan to reach new goals. The main goal for the helper in this step is to get the person back to a precrisis level of responding, not to work toward personality change or higher levels of growth. If the relationship continues, the helper may assist the person to gain perspectives on the crisis experience such that it stimulates renewed growth, for example, toward independence and self confidence.

Multiple Impact Support Strategy

Multiple impact strategy involves both an intensive and extensive support effort, usually combined with an active behavior change program. Teams of agencies and specialists generally are involved, each making an impact at the appropriate time and sequence. Environmental, or milieu, support is combined with relationship support. An example is a family in crisis that is given a minimum of two days' intensive round-the-clock attention in a residential, or family service center setting rather than in an agency, office, or the family's home. Thus, the family has the advantage of a fresh environment, a total medical-social-psychological approach, and individualized help in the form of group and interview work. The assumptions underlying this strategy are that a family in crisis must be helped as a unit, and that approaches to individual members would be ineffective. Total help in the early stages of a family crisis can be more effective than sporadic and progressive help later. The crisis can be used as a springboard for the family, or individuals therein, to mobilize resources to deal with the crisis and to grow. In this process they learn how to prevent future crises.

This same multiple strategy is used with independent adults who face a crisis not involving a family. They may go to a retreat setting, or to a one-day program in a community mental health center, and receive intensive attention from a variety of professional and nonprofessional helpers.

Building and Maintaining Hope

Since hopelessness, despair, and depression are such common components of stress and crisis, people depend heavily on helpers to deal constructively with these conditions. Hope is the main antidote to despair as well as the source of relief from tension and frustration of unmet goals. It grants some satisfaction to the person to feel that the future may bring this relief. As Korner (1970) has indicated, hope includes strong emotional components akin to faith. People "need them; they resist losing them; they fight to maintain them" (p. 136). To protect these fragile feelings, people develop a "rationalizing chain" that is "formed from bits of reality accompanied by and held together by logic and reasoning" (p. 137). When stress or crises come along, however, they are managed usually by strengthening the weak links with rationalizations. These rationalizations may clash increasingly with helpee perceptions of reality, until either they tighten the rationalizing logic in their chains or they revert to pure faith and feeling. Korner postulates a balanced condition, or "hope equation," between external sources of stress and a coping combination of faith and rationalizing that constitutes hope.

A first step in working with hope as a helping tool is to determine to what extent the nature and the degree of disturbance are in the feeling component, and to what extent in the rationalizing chain. If the feeling component is affected the person may be depressed, but is just as likely to have less visible feelings of hopelessness and the associated behaviors of passivity and detachment. In the case of sudden and severe loss, disorganization and dysfunction may be apparent.

After helpers have a better sense of their helpees' strengths, and how they are responding to the crisis, they can follow a general strategy of: (1) expression of feelings; (2) cognitive integration; (3) mobilization of resources; and (4) action. The goal of this strategy is for helpees to begin functioning minimally so that their deteriorative tendencies can be arrested and their strengths mobilized. The first step, then, is to get helpees talking about their feelings and hopes. If they feel helpless or numb, for example, let them talk about it. While it may assist helpees facing less severe stress to move quickly to step 2—to clarify their situations through rational discussion of their false logic, to examine possible alternatives, and to engage in problem-solving activities—this approach generally is not useful when the stress is severe and accompanied by feelings of intense hopelessness or helplessness. Ellis (1962) developed a step 2 cognitive approach that he labels *rational-emotive,* an attempt to examine the helpee's self-defeating and catastrophic logic. The idea is to look critically at the messages the helpee gives when he or she says, "I'm no good," "I'm a victim of circumstances," or "Isn't it awful?" If you wish to understand this approach to changing helpees' thinking about themselves and their situations, look at Ellis's work listed among the suggested readings at the end of the chapter.

Most initial efforts toward helping people build their hope structures are neither rational nor feeling oriented but are based on *action.* Loosening helpees from their lethargy and helpless feelings by encouraging activity aids their physical and mental well-being at this stage. Understanding skills should also be applied to provide an awareness of emotional support. The simple physical presence of a strong and understanding person as helpees talk about their feelings has some supportive effect. If these initial approaches fail to alter the despairing mood or passivity pattern, or if the condition seems to be deteriorating into feeling and thought disorders (delusion, hallucination, paranoia, fixed and unreal ideas), emergency referral measures would be appropriate.

In the specialized setting of a crisis center hotline, one study on effectiveness of direct advice compared with empathic listening strongly suggested that callers' immediate preferences were for the direct advice approach. This approach was preferred over a combination of approaches offered by paraprofessional helpers (Libow and Doty 1976). One implication of findings such as these is that helpers dealing with crises must be prepared with a variety of approaches, including offering direct suggestions.

When helpees begin moving from their helpless feelings and passive behaviors, they can examine the "lost faith" and/or the missing links in their "rationalizing chain." The main helping strategy at this stage is to continue understanding support. Helpers should watch for opportunities to reinforce renewed hope, but they should also be aware of the limitations of too much approval of what the helpee is thinking and feeling. The choices about direction of the helpees' renewable belief system or reconstituted logic should be theirs, since these are value decisions. What should be reinforced is their effort to renew their hope.

The other option that helpees face at this juncture is to stop thinking about hoping temporarily and to face the situation or causes of the crisis directly. Or they may construct new hope structures better suited to their needs for security and more functional for controlling their anxiety. Regardless of which of the three options they choose, helpees need much supportive understanding at this stage. They need encouragement of efforts to reestablish their equilibrium and adaptive strength, as well as to act as responsibly as possible in this crisis. When helpees reach this stage of mastery in resolution of their crises, they are in a position to explore renewal steps described in the next strategy. A significant factor in maintaining hope is the constant reminder that out of crises come new growth and opportunity for renewal.

Strategy of Renewal and Growth

Renewal and growth strategy is aimed primarily at identifying strengths in people, helping them to be aware of these strengths, and then helping them to develop a plan for releasing these growth potentials. It is not a strategy designed for helpees still in a state of crisis, however, because it "pushes" people into disequilibrium as a prelude to growth. This strategy requires skills in strength analysis and a whole array of competencies for facilitating awareness.

Much renewal work is done in the hundreds of residential growth centers and institutes in the United States alone. These centers are not associated with formal educational structures, and they operate in a fairly unstructured fashion without courses, grades, or credits. Much use is made of encounter groups, sensory awareness, gestalt integration, communications training, meditation, and creative arts. A retreat setting facilitates concentration on developing the new skills and experiences apart from the realities and pressures of daily life. A laboratory approach enables the person to try out new experiences in the protected atmosphere of the group or growth center community without the risks inherent in real life settings. The feedback under conditions of trust and safety is an invaluable contribution to personal growth. Participants establish their own growth goals and use the resources of the center to reach them. Renewal groups, for example, offer opportunities to reflect on values and purposes as well as to explore alternative life styles and to discover hidden potentials.

Although a helper may want to refer someone to such a growth center, these renewal and growth strategies are very specialized and, in some cases, experimental. Usually, they require the helpee to take some personal risks. Therefore, such strategies are not considered basic helping skills.

For the helpee who has weathered a crisis and is at the stage of rebuilding, referral to such renewal groups reinforces hopes and strengths. The helpee experiences the warmth and support that come about from trusting others who are themselves on the personal growth quest.

The limitations of this movement, however, are that its popularity has attracted many helping opportunists who are poorly qualified to facilitate such educational experiences. There are few effective ways to control abuses and destructive outcomes of such irresponsible growth efforts. Like so many potential aids, this growth movement has side effects and misuses, as does use of medicinal drugs. It is a case of "let the buyer beware"; so it is essential to check carefully into the reputation of the growth center as well as into the backgrounds of the leaders before urging helpees to utilize this opportunity for renewal.

Then too the leader may be highly skilled and may have an esteemed reputation, but the experience could be inappropriate for this helpee at this time. All helpers, therefore, need to become familiar, preferably in firsthand experience, with the possibilities and limitations of various styles of renewal opportunities. Howard (1970), for example, has reported on her year of explorations of these various growth experiences and cites her reactions to the centers, leaders, and styles of groups. Her book is a good starting place for those who are unfamiliar with growth groups.

The Crisis Center

For the helpee faced with continuing stress expressed as suicide attempts, drug abuse, or assault, the multiple approaches of a team of helpers often are needed. Most large communities now have such centers supported by community chests, private foundations, or public funds. Many are experimental efforts to meet community crises. They usually combine medical, psychological, and casework resources with peer helpers and volunteers. Examples are drug crisis clinics and suicide prevention centers. Even Travelers' Aid, long concerned with people in distress, has been thrust increasingly into the crisis effort. Many centers operate telephone crisis lines that the person facing acute stress can call for supportive help and referral information by phone.

The Halfway House

The halfway house resource utilizes a strategy of facilitating transition from the crisis center or treatment facility to real life. Such houses are usually small homelike places with resident helping persons. The goal is to provide a semiprotected residential atmosphere where coping mechanisms and personality strengths can be developed before the helpee faces the demands of the real world. As the name implies, it is a facility halfway between the protective institution, or clinic, and the normal community. Work-release programs from prisons have the same rationale.

The Treatment Center

Treatment centers vary from the total environmental control of the conventional hospital, day-care center, and community mental hygiene clinic to small homelike residential centers. An example of a residential center is Synanon, which focuses on drug rehabilitation performed by those who have been abusers of drugs but who have now adopted a different life style and are willing to assist others who want to change their style of coping with stress without the use of drugs.

Another example is the camp or farm for teenagers who cannot cope with the stress of family and community demands. The Achievement Place (Phillips et al. 1971) in Kansas is an experimental program for teenage boys who are in trouble with the law and with their families. It is a residential environment that shapes behavior through a point system of rewards and support. A similar program, called Learning House (Thoreson 1971), is designed for children ages three through twelve who are having trouble in home or school. They are taken from their home environments for short periods to the special reward-controlled environment of the Learning House to relearn more adaptive forms of behavior.

Therapeutic Counseling Strategy

Most of the strategies described above involve multiple approaches in environmentally controlled settings. Much of the helping process for people under stress or in crisis takes place in one-to-one interview formats, commonly labeled counseling. The usual strategy in counseling is to open the interview systematically with clarification of the reasons for the helpee's coming, establish mutual goals and responsibilities, then carry out a plan of action to reach the helpee's goals, and finally terminate the relationship. The counseling process varies according to the assumptions of the counselor about how behavior is changed and how personal problems are solved. Chapter 7 cites examples of these varying styles. Some counselors, such as Frankl (1965), use an existential framework that focuses on the meaning of existence. They see helping as a process of assisting helpees search for meaning in their existence and helping them to put tragedy and suffering in perspective. This "will to meaning" is not the same as faith or hope; it is a way of coping with the tension between what a person is and what he or she could become. "Logotherapy," as Frankl describes his view, is a means for dealing with the meaninglessness many persons feel about their lives and focuses on changing the way people construe their existence as a way of confronting directly the anxiety of living. Corliss and Rabe (1969) describe and illustrate in more detail this style of helping people through crises.

Behavioral counseling approaches, on the other hand, focus on helping people to change the environments that shape their behavior. It is concerned with behavior that leads to the feelings of discomfort and the consequences of acts to relieve that distress. Comfort derives from feelings of mastery over self and environment. Behavioral counseling writers have had little to say about utilizing crises, except in a general problem-solving framework.

Consoling Strategy

Consoling strategy is the traditional ministerial approach to comfort and crisis utilization and involves more than simple therapeutic counseling. For those persons who respond to religious ritual, writings, and assurances of life after death, it is a powerful supportive strategy, particularly in times of bereavement. Childhood beliefs are reincorporated into the rational chain, and faith reestablishes hope. The person of the pastor has a supportive effect also through whatever associations of strength and protection are made to him. This religious tie may be some helpees' only means of managing grief so that they can move quickly through the grief process to new levels of growth and strength. Americans facing stress and crises still depend to a high degree on religiously oriented helpers (Gurin et al. 1960).

Skills for Comfort and Crisis Utilization

It is difficult to speak of special skills for creating conditions of comfort. As indicated earlier in the chapter, comfort is due largely to the personal qualities transmitted by the helper. Just being with the helpee in an attentive way during periods of stress is comforting. Thus, almost all the skills for understanding also convey support and result in comfort. Listening to the helpee ventilate feelings, for example, has a powerfully supportive effect. Similarly the skills for action to be described in the next chapter have implications for helping people move from passivity, so often characteristic of people in crisis, to action in building new relationships and planning for the future. The following skills can be used as supplements for those described earlier to produce conditions of comfort and to make use of the growth potential of crises.

Contacting Skills

Chapter 4 described *eye contact* as an essential ingredient in attending to the helpee. This nonphysical contact reassures helpees that the helper is with them. Physical *touch,* as we all know from our experiences with our families and friends, is another form of contact that has powerful comforting qualities. Among helpers, however, the question of touching helpees is very controversial. Putting a hand on a pupil's shoulder as a gesture of support and perhaps affection by teachers is considered inappropriate by many helpers and parents. Americans seem to have strong touch taboos not present in many other societies. Even though we recognize the power of touch to comfort, and even though many helpers favor its use, they must regard touch as a high risk method at the present time. The decision to touch depends on the context and structure of the helping relationship. Touching is more permissible in the informal helping situation because it is more akin to friendship, where touching is encouraged.

Touch should be used with discretion, after consideration of agency policy, and the age and sex of the helpee. Holding a helpee's hand, or putting a firm hand on the person's arm or shoulder while he or she is struggling with a painful feeling can be most helpful to comfort or to facilitate further exploration. Embracing or sitting on laps, for example, would be a high risk behavior considering present mores; but, again, under present circumstances of rapid cultural change, it might be the appropriate thing to do for the helpee's benefit. When using physical contact it is important that helpers have a high degree of awareness of their own needs for contact and are sufficiently in touch with their own feelings so they can be perceptive about the helpees' needs and reactions to their contacting skills. In other words, the foremost question to be answered is, Whose needs are being served? We should be alert, for example, to helpees whose experiences with the opposite sex and close human relationships generally have been so restricted that they react with intense anxiety to any kind of physical contact. There are reported instances where helper contact has been misinterpreted to the point where accusations of seduction or molestation have been made. Some of these claims were probably justified as unethical behavior, but some were undoubtedly misjudgments of the helper about the nature of trust and mutual acceptance present. This contact issue must be decided finally on the bases of: (1) the good judgment of the helper about the needs of this helpee; (2) helpers' awareness of their own needs and ethics; (3) what is likely to be most helpful within the helper's rationale of helping; and (4) what risks the helper is willing to take, having considered agency policy, local custom, professional ethics, and age, sex, and attitude of the helpee.

Reassuring Skills

Reassurance is a method of verbally assuring helpees about the consequences of their actions or feelings. It acts as a reward since it reduces stress and builds confidence, and also fosters expectancies of future rewards. Examples of reassuring comments and suggestions are, "You are competent," "You can be reasonable," "You can solve your problem." "You can feel better." The goals of using reassurance are to increase helpees' confidence, mobilize their strengths, reduce their anxiety to optimum working levels, or reinforce a desired behavior.

One reassuring skill is *expressing approval* of a helpee's statement. You say, for example, "That sounds to me like a good idea—very thoughtful." This process of agreeing, of course, reinforces helpees' expressions. Paradoxically, reassurance tends to fix the stated idea; the helpee, as a consequence, is less likely to change that idea or behavior.

A second reassuring skill is *predicting outcomes.* The helper says, for example, "You have been exploring your feelings pretty intensively today. You really have been spilling it out the last few minutes and now we have to go. You'll probably find yourself a bit moody the next couple of days; but this happens frequently, so don't worry about it." Another example is, "You have had a tough adjustment to face with your father's death, and it will probably continue to be rough for awhile; but you will be able to handle it all right."

A third use of reassuring skill is *factual assurance.* Telling helpees that their problems have solutions, that people with this kind of difficulty make it, or that annoying symptoms disappear at fairly predictable times, enables them to tolerate the momentary stress. Reassurance can be given at an even more specific factual level, such as assuring them that there are known steps to formulate sound career plans or to improve study performance.

Some of the *limitations* and *cautions* in using reassurance are: (1) It is easy to use, so there is a temptation to *overuse* it. (2) It may cause *hostility* in the helpee who may feel the true nature of some serious condition was concealed or minimized. Helpees may feel that the helper is *minimizing* the seriousness of their feelings by remarks that indicate that "Everything will come out all right" or "It isn't as bad as you think it is." (3) Reassurance efforts come across often as insincere *sympathy,* which may jeopardize the whole helping relationship. (4) *Dependency* is often encouraged by use of reassurance because people need periodic doses, which then act as a mechanism for avoiding change in their behavior. (5) If the reassurance is interpreted as agreement, helpees may feel *trapped* in their present thinking and action.

In summary, guidelines for reassurance are:

1. Depend mainly on the positive quality of the relationship for supportive reassurance rather than relying on verbal forms of assurance.
2. Use verbal reassurance mainly to reduce distress through facts and predictions.
3. Use reassurance sparingly as a reinforcing agent to encourage continuing behaviors.

Relaxing Skills

Since stress is usually accompanied by physical tension, one of the most direct forms of inducing comfort is to work directly on muscle tension. There are a number of styles of inducing relaxation through direct suggestion. Jacobson (1938) has a form of progressive relaxation that systematically induces relaxation in large muscle groups by alternating the tensing and releasing of these muscles. Some practitioners have put their induction methods on tape; Lazarus's (1971) recording is an example. Inducing relaxation is a simple skill to learn, and it has few hazards. Occasionally, hypersuggestible persons appear to go into a kind of hypnotic state, which may become a problem for the beginning helper. Simply telling helpees that when you finish counting to five they will wake up usually is sufficient.

Other ways to induce relaxation are simple focusing on breathing, even counting slowly on inhaling and slowly on exhaling. One limitation in such prolonged efforts is a condition called "hyperventilation" where the person may feel momentarily dizzy or faint after breathing too deeply. Certain body positions, such as those advocated in Yoga, induce relaxation also. Vocalizations, such as chants, sighing deeply, and repeating expansive sounds, such as "a-ohm," help some people to relax. States of awareness, or consciousness, advocated by Zen practitioners also promote ease and physical relaxation. Hot baths with fast moving water have been used for millenia to induce relaxation. Since a detailed discussion of relaxation methods is beyond the scope of this chapter, helpers who desire to use these skills in their helping relationships should read basic works on physical relaxation, and the Eastern Zen and Yoga writers on awareness and meditation.

The *uses* of relaxation skills are varied. They may be used as a primary method to produce relief from tension precipitated by stressful conditions. Helpees frequently react with gratitude at the rapidity of relief that is afforded and thus feel more confidence in your ability to help them. Relaxation methods can be applied when you wish to reduce their anxiety and physical tension to sufficiently tolerable limits so that verbal skills can be utilized for understanding, comfort, or action. Relaxation methods also are part of the sequence of systematic desensitization, a method for changing behavior to be described in the next chapter.

Guidelines on relaxing skills are:

1. Learn a verbally induced relaxation method that is comfortable for you.
2. Learn the importance of focusing on breathing as a quick relaxation method.
3. Become familiar with various psychological forms of relaxation as practiced by Eastern mystics, as an adjunct to your physical relaxation methods.

Centering Skills Cluster

Development of centering comfort skills assumes that the helper regards the human personality as something beyond a collection of its components. Centering is a process of getting "in touch" and then "in tune" with one's person, or total self. Centering results in awareness of peace, harmony, unity, and strength. This skill cluster shows how different helpers emphasize different skills, depending on their personal experiences and assumptions about human personality. The helper has to view people as having an area in their psyches of private experiencing, called the "center," or the core of their being.

There are a variety of helper styles of centering and correcting overemphasis on one modality of existence, such as thinking. One is a progressive awareness process where the helper tells helpees to close their eyes, get comfortable, and breath slowly and deeply. Then the helper goes through a few verbal suggestions to guide their awareness to the center of being. Say, for example, "Your body is part of you . . . but your body is not the total you; what else is there? You have feelings; they are part of you . . . , but your feelings are not the total you. What else is there? You are a thinking being; you have ideas . . . , but your thoughts are not the total you. You have a center where all of these parts of you come together, a center of your being where you experience peace, wholeness, strength . . . ; this center is an important part of you. . . ."

Centering methods such as this one are used to help people who feel out of tune, or even at war with themselves. Parts of their personalities are working at cross-purposes and consuming enormous amounts of energy. Their bodies, for example, may be out of phase with their thoughts. The aim is to promote an awareness of smoothness and unity as a means toward comfort. The method is designed also to get the parts back into balance. Some helpees, for example, seem to have exaggerated awareness and valuing of their bodies to the exclusion of other phases of existence. Conversely, people who have denied body experience find great comfort in rediscovering their bodies and the feelings locked in their muscles. In crisis situations, helpees are comforted to realize that the center of their being is a place where they can find peace and strength. This experience of centering has great survival value for our society.

In this context, Corliss and Rabe (1969) speak of two modes of being, peripheral and central. The person existing at the *peripheral* level is concerned primarily with doing, with changing the physical world, whereas the *centrally* oriented person focuses more on internal personal states of feelings, dreams, wishes, and intuitions. The "center" exists more in fantasy; it is a place of quietude and receptivity. A key problem of living is maintaining an effective balance between these two modes of existence. The helping strategy involved in working through crises of life style is to lead persons through an analysis of values associated with peripheral living and help them to center their existence. Then the helper facilitates helpee choices with decision skills cited in the next chapter and with communication skills described in the preceding chapter.

Strength analysis is also a method of centering, although it operates more as a descriptive device to build strength and confidence. It is applicable to nonstress situations as well and is a form of building strength to utilize future crises constructively. In this method the helper simply asks helpees to focus on their strong points and to list them out loud. It may be a matter of only three or four points, but they are usually sufficient to start helpees thinking of their positive strengths. In periods of stress the usual tendency is to focus on weak and negative personal qualities and to exaggerate them. Self-abnegation and criticism often accompany depressed moods. This method of strength analysis is *not* a method of reassuring the person that she or he is strong and capable or suggesting that "Every day in every way, you're getting better and better." The list of strengths, with specific examples, comes from the helpee.

Reviewing growth experiences is a method of asking the helpee to focus on pleasant or unpleasant experiences (the more recent, the better) that have had a profoundly positive effect on growth. This request is often interpreted to mean traumatic events that have had a frustrating or negative effect, but these may be dealt with productively at another time. The helpee's focus here must be on events that had positive outcomes. This process leads to reexperiencing feelings long outside of awareness. The effect is strengthening helpees' images of themselves as capable persons with the strength to meet stress and crisis. They can point to specific instances where they have done so in the past.

Reviewing peak experiences has an effect similar to the growth experience analysis above. In chapter 1, we discussed Maslow's term peak experience to mean those life experiences, usually short and infrequent, when the person is aware of intense pleasure, exhilaration, joy, and fulfillment. Recalling and focusing on such experiences can be rewarding in terms of comfort and satisfaction.

Crisis Intervening Skills

Crisis intervening skills are a cluster of skills, most of which have been described in other contexts. These skills induce comfort through support and understanding, or through altering the helpees' response by a change in their environment. The skills of building hope, contact through touching, and comfort through empathic listening apply to crisis situations. Supportive actions through changed living arrangements and sedative drugs are additional methods used by specialists to alter the helpee's environment. The presence of a warm and understanding person, not personally involved with the crisis, is very supportive. Referral methods for special forms of help are part of the crisis intervention cluster also.

Developing Action Alternatives

One of the characteristics of people in crisis is a narrowing of perception—that is, they see very few solutions or alternatives. "Suicide is my only way out" is an example. One of the skill clusters to help such people is to encourage them to consider alternatives through suggesting some possibilities, as well as by drawing ideas from the helpee. The helping goals are to facilitate a realistic perception of the crisis event, provide support to reduce the tensions associated with the crisis or conflict, consider all the coping alternatives, and then make a commitment to action to achieve reasonable equilibrium and comfort.

The idea of equilibrium in crisis theory espoused by Aguilera and Messick (1974) states that people seek an emotional equilibrium between their problems and possible solutions. When their coping skills are inadequate, or their action alternatives are too narrow, they experience inner tension or distress, which, when severe, forms the crisis. Part of the helper's task is to assist the person to avoid abortive solutions to his or her problems during the crisis until the person's coping mechanisms are revitalized.

Referring Skills

At times even the most skilled and confident helpers admit frustration and defeat in dealing with persons in crisis. Referral is one approach where the helpee can have a fresh start. For the beginning helper, referral is a common method of managing crisis conditions in helpees. Although referral seems a simple skill, these specific methods make it more effective:

1. Know community resources for different kinds of services.
2. Explore helpee readiness for referral. Have they expressed interest in specialized help? Are they afraid of seeing a "shrink"? Do we frighten them with implications of the severity of their problems, such as the inflection we give to, "You had better see a psychiatrist!"?
3. Be direct and honest about your observations of their behavior that led to your suggested referral. Be honest also about your own limitations. If after working with them for awhile, you feel that it would be in their best interest to receive more intensive help from a specialist, you might say something like, "Let's explore what other possible resources would be available for help with this question." This illustrative statement does not imply they are too disturbed or confused for you to handle and therefore must be in *really* bad shape.
4. It is usually desirable to discuss the possibility of referral with the referral agency before the problem becomes urgent.
5. Determine what other persons have had contact with this helpee and confer with them before suggesting further steps.
6. If the helpee is a minor it is wise to inform the parents of your recommendations and obtain their consent and cooperation.
7. Be fair in explaining the services of a referral agency by citing the possibilities and the limitations of that agency. Do not imply that miracles can be performed there.
8. Let the helpee or the helpee's parent make their own appointments for the new service, although sometimes supportive services like offering transportation would be facilitative.

9. Do not release information to any referral source without written permission from helpees or their parents in the form of a signed release.

10. If you have been having the primary helping relationship with the helpee, it is only ethical to maintain that relationship until the referral is complete and a new relationship is begun.

Renewing or Building Support Systems

Mentioned earlier under steps in crisis intervention was the necessity to facilitate the person's linkage to a support system. Such a system provides the encouragement, love, and security so desired immediately by persons suffering loss. Later, a support system provides reality checks on expectations of others and honest feedback on one's behavior—so difficult to get from the larger community. Examples of support groups are families, clubs, close neighborhood groups, church organizations, and groups of friends specifically organized as a support group. This type of support goes beyond the friendly ear of a close associate or relative. A close-knit family group is probably the best source of such support when the self-destructive forces of loss impinge on a person. Persons in crisis desperately need refurbishing of their feelings of personal worth and an opportunity to check reality perceptions until they have mobilized their own resources to go on.

The principal problem with groups such as those above is that they often do not function for the person, either because the person in crisis has no connection with such a primary group, or because the group extracts a price of conformity to its norms and values as a condition of offering support. Helpers need to know community resources for different helping situations. In many communities, groups such as widows' lifelines or divorce lifelines offer help to those without family support groups and also supplement the help of groups such as families and neighbors. The suggested readings at the end of this chapter offer further ideas on using developing support systems.

Expected Outcomes

Now that you have studied this chapter you can: (1) describe and illustrate the terms *stress, crisis, support, hope,* and *grief*; (2) describe and illustrate eight helping strategies for dealing with stress and crisis; (3) list three skills from the chapter on understanding that have supportive effects also; (4) describe two arguments for and against contacting, reassuring, and relaxing skills; (5) list ten principles for referral of helpees to other persons or agencies. The final outcome to be expected is your ability to apply these methods and principles such that helpees feel and act in ways that indicate confidence and comfort.

Suggestions for Further Study

BENSON, A., *Relaxation Response.* New York: William Morrow, 1975.

BRAMMER, L., and SHOSTROM, E., *Therapeutic Psychology.* 3rd ed. Englewood Cliffs, N.J.: Prentice-Hall, 1977. (Ch. 6 on support functions, ch. 7 on reassurance methods, and ch. 15 on value problems.)

CAPLAN, G., and KILLILEA, M., eds., *Support Systems and Mutual Help.* New York: Grune & Stratton, 1976. (A collection of procedures and descriptions of exemplary programs of support for organizing support systems.)

CORLISS, R., and RABE, P., *Psychotherapy from the Center: A Humanistic View of Change and Growth.* Scranton, Pa.: International Textbook, 1969. (An existential view of counseling strategy.)

ELLIS, A., *Reason and Emotion in Psychotherapy.* Secaucus, N.J.: Lyle Stuart, 1962. (A method of helping people in crisis look at their illogical thinking.)

FARBER, M., *A Theory of Suicide.* New York: Funk & Wagnalls, 1968. (An analysis of the experience of suicide prevention centers.)

FEIFEL, H., *The Meaning of Death.* New York: McGraw-Hill, 1959. (A psychological approach to death and dying.)

GARDNER, J., *Self-renewal.* New York: Harper & Row, 1963. (A short essay on the necessity for renewing individuals and changing institutions.)

HOWARD, J., *Please Touch.* New York: McGraw-Hill, 1970. (A newswoman's report of a year in various growth centers.)

KÜBLER-ROSS, E., *On Death and Dying.* New York: Macmillan, 1969. (Psychological issues and methods for dealing with death.)

———, *Death: The Final Stage of Growth.* Englewood Cliffs, N.J.: Prentice-Hall, 1975.

LAMOTT, K., *Escape from Stress.* New York: Berkley, 1975.

LESTER, G., and LESTER, D., *Suicide: The Gamble with Death.* Englewood Cliffs, N.J.: Prentice-Hall, 1971. (A broad behavioral science study of suicide.)

LINDEMANN, E., "Symptomatology and management of acute grief." *American Journal of Psychiatry* 101 (1944); 7–21. Reprinted in Parad, H. *Crisis Intervention: Selected Readings,* ch. 1. (Practical suggestions for managing extreme loss reactions.)

MARIN, P., and COHEN, A., *Understanding Drug Use.* New York: Harper & Row, 1971. (An adult's guide to drugs and the young.)

PARAD, H., *Crisis Intervention: Selected Readings.* New York: Family Service Association of America, 1965. (A collection of reprints on grief, family crises, maternal reactions, school entry, relocation, illness, and psychiatric crises.)

SIX

Helping Skills for Positive Action and Behavior Change

People come to helpers mainly because they are unhappy about some aspect of their behavior. Although they do not always state their goal as wanting to change a specific behavior, like shyness, they soon see that their actions must be the ultimate focus of their attention. Essentially, all helping is aimed toward action outcomes of some kind. If specific actions are involved, the process is described usually as behavior modification. This process of changing behavior applies not only to observable actions but also to covert or internal behavior, such as how people think of themselves, how they feel about other people, or how they view their world. These internal states are determined from verbal self-reports, but we look for specific actions to verify them. For example, we look for positive self-descriptions if they feel good about themselves. By observing actions, such as the degree of assertive social behavior exhibited by helpees, we can infer how confident they feel about themselves when they are around others.

A positive action approach gives helpers specific evidence that they have been helpful according to the extent that their helpees have reached their goals. There is much discussion about *accountability* in all helping agencies. Before proceeding, ask yourself what the term accountability means to you—accountability to whom and for what outcomes? Accountability means that you, as the helper, assume a large share of responsibility to meet specific behavioral outcomes of the helping process. It means also that you look for evidence that the helpee is achieving the goals determined in the early stages of the helping process described in chapter 3. An action program in an accountability framework, means that the helpee was involved extensively in both establishing and assessing the objectives.

Positive action refers to two types of processes that will form the remaining content of this chapter. One is a problem-solving and decision-making cluster of processes and skills. The other cluster of skills is aimed at changing specific kinds of behaviors, usually by acquiring a skill rather than removing a deficiency. Some examples of the kinds of concerns brought to helpers that have specific skill involvement are improving study skills, acquiring social skills, developing more assertive behaviors, and diminishing unnecessary fears. Essentially, the helper is in the position of a teacher of skills for solving problems, changing behavior, and achieving higher levels of functioning.

There are practically unlimited possibilities for improving human capacities. Numerous writers on the human potential estimate that we use about 10 percent of our potentialities. Studies underway on control of body functions, particularly brain powers, will open vast reservoirs of energy and action potential. Various methods of monitoring our own behavior, controlling negative thoughts, improving self-images, and altering our consciousness at will are not too far off. Helpers skilled in teaching others how to manage their own behavior through knowledge of behavior-changing and problem-solving skills will have a powerful helping resource.

Persons both in and out of the helping framework have mixed feelings about, and sometimes even totally reject, the behavior modification approach. Some equate it to "brainwashing," and others see it as the "salvation of society." These methods *are* powerful techniques for changing behavior that can be misapplied by unscrupulous people. This is a problem analogous to using chemicals to alter behavior for better or for worse. These behavior changing methods can enhance helpees' freedom in many ways by expanding their options for response. They can determine their own goals, and they can choose the methods used to achieve those goals; so the issue is not whether the processes and skills have good or evil in themselves, but whether they are used in an ethical or unethical manner. The basic problem is not *whether* the helpee's behavior will be controlled, but *by whom* and *for whose benefit.* Behavior modification is a technology, not an ethical system.

Outcomes You Can Expect

The purpose of this chapter is to examine the processes and skills that will accomplish the helping functions described above. It focuses on acting and changing observable behavior, whereas the preceding two chapters emphasized more subtle changes in social attitude, self-regard, and perception of life circumstances. As a result of studying this chapter you will have competencies to: (1) describe the steps in a problem-solving and decision-making model of helping; (2) apply relevant skills in appropriate sequences; (3) describe and illustrate skills for changing behavior such as modeling, contracting, rewarding, extinguishing, desensitizing, and aversion controlling.

Although it is unrealistic to expect to apply these skills expertly after reading about them, it is reasonable for you to expect to try them out with understanding and to evaluate your success with them. Since you will have specific outcomes to observe, these skills should be easier to evaluate than those described in previous chapters. A note of caution, though: these behavior modification skills appear deceptively simple to apply, yet they require practice and feedback from those who are specialized in behavior modification methods. After you study the methods here and in the suggested readings, find a setting in which you can try these skills under supervision of a behavioral change specialist.

Characteristics and Assumptions of the Action Approach to Helping

Characteristics

The main focus in the action approach is on changing *specific helpee behaviors,* whereas the focus in the two preceding chapters has been on general goals and on changing perceptions and feelings as intermediate goals. Whereas change in behavior is the ultimate standard for judging success of all helping styles, the action approach places special stress on helpee behavioral outcomes. Action methods are characterized by an objective empirical approach to helpee goals and environmental change.

Action approaches come under the helping strategy called behavioral counseling. The principal characteristics of this strategy are: (1) careful *assessment* of the helpee's problem behavior and conditions that maintain that behavior; (2) agreement on precise *goals* for new behaviors; (3) application mainly of *change skills* described below but utilization of all helping skills; (4) evaluation of *outcomes* in relation to goals; (5) *feedback* information to improve the process. Behavioral counseling strategists stress the importance of learning problem-solving methods so that self-directed action can take place in everyday problem situations.

Behavioral helpers look at the helpee's present behavior and the complex environment in which it takes place. Thus, the helper takes minimum notice of psychological traits and problems. Some behavioral helpers, especially in working with children, get a baseline count of the child's undesirable and desirable behaviors before doing anything else. This count gives them a basis for judging the effectiveness of the help in terms of decreases of undesirable and increases in desirable behavior.

Assumptions

Behavior is the result of interactive external environmental forces and internal heredity forces. Continued responses are the result of learning by imitation and reward. Behavior is mediated somewhat by thinking processes, also, and is not only an automatic response to a rewarding environment. Social learning is a function of the interaction between the person's early behavior patterns and controlling environmental social conditions. The basic framework for action helping methods is the social learning approach described by Bandura (1969). Although the environment has profound impact on people's behavior, sometimes their behavior also alters the social environment considerably.

The use of behavior change methods assumes that helpees come for expert help in changing a specific behavior and are not seeking supportive friendly relationships or an examination of their value commitments. Such help, covered in previous chapters, is not suited to the behavior technology approaches described below.

Implications

Some implications of the action approach for the helping process are that helper and helpee try to establish goals, find solutions, and make plans together. As a helper, you will use a variety of methods to assist the helpee to achieve specific goals. You will be responsible to observe what is happening at all times so that you can define in concrete ways what progress, if any, the two of you are making toward the helpee's goals. While you will trust your judgment and feelings about what is going on, you will look for specific outcomes to check your hunches. By being very specific with the helpee about concrete outcomes, you keep vagueness and mysticism out of the helping process. You say, for example, "I agreed to work with you, but you need to do some work outside of our talk sessions because what you do out there is the important payoff of our work here. We will be talking about very concrete things you can do to help your situation out there, and we will want to look occasionally at the progress we are making."

This action approach is not an emotionally sterile and strictly rational procedure, as is often claimed. Action methods work very effectively in a relationship characterized by the facilitative conditions described in chapter 2. Mickelson and Stevic (1971) found that behaviorally oriented counselors with high warmth, empathy, and genuineness were more effective in generating information-seeking responses in their helpees than those behavioral counselors rated low on facilitative conditions.

Problems and Goals

Since action outcomes are our concern, it is very important to identify specific problems and translate those problems into precise goals. Helpees seldom come with neatly stated problems. They usually are expressed in vague feelings of confusion, dissatisfaction, or distress. Often complaints are focused on another person or institution. Thus, helpers begin, as in other styles of helping, with listening for understanding. They try to communicate this understanding, and often this is enough for the helpee to feel understood and comforted. But if the helper's listening reveals that the helpee needs to *act* differently, another strategy is needed. As the helpers listen they are gaining information about the specifics in helpees' lives—how they look at themselves and others, what they want, and what their environment is like. From these data about the helpee's initial complaints and feelings, the helper and helpee together *describe* how he *acts now* and how he would *like to act*. Thus, *goals* are formulated toward which he can work with some help from the helper in the form of suggested methods. Goals, according to Krumboltz (1966), must meet three criteria: (1) the goals are desired by the helpee and tailored to him; (2) the helper is willing to help him work toward the goal; (3) attainment of the goal is observable and assessable. Krumboltz emphasizes that general goals, such as "self-understanding" and "self-actualization," are accepted by almost everyone, but to be useful in an action approach they must be stated in the unique and specific language of the helpee. An example of such a specific action goal is, "I want to avoid crying every time I am criticized." This goal implies that helpees will understand why they cry, but it goes beyond understanding and relief of distress to the action of changing crying behavior.

Krumboltz's second criterion, willingness of the helper, is significant because the goals of the helpee must fit the ethical, legal, and competency requirements of the helper. For example, it would not be appropriate for a helper to be a party to a helpee's scheme to cheat on an examination or take advantage of a weaker person, even though it were very important to the helpee to do so. Helpers should always have the option of refusing help if they feel the goals are questionable.

Difficulties in Stating Goals

Changing helpee problems into specific goals with observable outcomes is one of the principal difficulties in the action approach. Some of the difficulties cited by Krumboltz and Thoreson (1976) are as follows.

1. It is important to determine who the helpee is. This problem was discussed in chapter 3 under the second process stage—clarification. The following brief example will illustrate the problem in this special context. If a parent refers a child for counseling, it is easy to be confused about who needs help—the parent or the child. The helpee is defined as the one who brings the problem to the helper, since for the time being, at least, that person "owns" the problem. Although the helper may understand the plight of the person who is trying to bring another person in for help, sometimes it is necessary to say firmly, "Let's discuss how I might help you deal with this person so you can help him to change his behavior." You, as a helper, may still want to see the other person, but at least you have established a helping partnership with the referring person and are not carrying the full responsibility for a most difficult helping situation.

2. Helpees *express their problems as feelings,* such as, "I am miserable," "I am lonely," or "I am frustrated." After applying the skills for understanding to help clarify the feeling statements, Krumboltz and Thoreson suggest a further approach: ask the helpee, "What could you *do* to make yourself wanted, attractive, or loved by other persons?" The assumption here is that helpees need to take action counter to the feeling expressed to gain the response they want—love, respect, or money, for example. This step may mean acquiring a new competency.

Another problem faced by helpers is people with high aspirations who set unrealistic standards, continually comparing themselves to other of extraordinary competence. Furthermore, such people assume their feelings of incompetence or loneliness are unique because they seldom share these feelings and have little basis for judging the realism of their feelings. Help in this situation consists mainly of receiving accurate information about others' feelings, making realistic plans for achievement, and accepting the reality of the frustration and disillusionment.

3. *Lack of a goal* and not knowing their own desires can be a source of difficulty for helpees. Krumboltz and Thoreson point out that such helpees must come to realize that values and goals are not discovered but are created by people for themselves. Thus, the most helpful thing one can do with such "purposeless and alienated" people is to encourage them to construct goals for *their* lives or to adopt goals of other groups—religious, political, social, service—to give purpose to their existence. Most people need some large purpose or cause to give meaning and zest to their lives. The general helping strategy is to engage them in an active, exploratory process where they try on different goals and organizational identities until they find some that match their vaguely defined desires.

4. Desired *goals may be inappropriate or unclear.* Helpees may want to do something that, in your opinion, is against their best interests. If we really believe that they must make their own decisions, the most we can do is offer our opinions as additional information they can consider. It is best if our opinion is solicited. Sometimes helpees give helpers biased views, so helpers cannot get a clear idea of the helpees' problem. Helpees may not know why their behavior is disliked or unacceptable; an example is the teenager who says others do not like her and she cannot tell why. The general helping strategy is to encourage her to note what she is doing to make herself unwanted and to set goals for trying new behaviors that make her more attractive to others.

5. *Choice conflict* also makes it difficult to set behavioral goals. A common condition brought to helpers is one in which all the choices are unacceptable or unattainable. An example is the couple who want separation to resolve their conflict, yet do not want the financial problems associated with a divorce. The general helping strategy is to decide whether the helpee needs to learn problem-solving skills or to explore the full range of alternatives. In any case, the helper must confront helpees with the necessity to pin down goals, such as exploring all the possible consequences of each choice facing them.

6. Sometimes helpees have *no real problem,* but just want to talk. They do not want an action goal. Helpers then must decide if they want to spend their time in this manner or suggest that their helpees find someone else to talk with.

Moving Beyond Goals

We have been discussing some of the difficulties of translating problems into specific goal statements that make sense to the helpee. Once the goals have been agreed on, the skill of contracting is used to determine how, when and by whom the goal-seeking efforts will be initiated and maintained. The process of comparing results against the goals is a continuous one, so helpers know when they are succeeding. If the helpee is not moving toward the mutually determined goals at a reasonable rate, a diagnostic inquiry must be started to answer the question, Why not? Then a corrective procedure can be instituted.

Finally, the process is evaluated to see what can be learned that will make helping for action strategies more successful. Evaluation of helpee outcomes against specific goals for action also makes accountability for performing the helping tasks much easier to demonstrate. Those helpers working in an agency context are finding this evaluative function a political necessity for survival as well as a continuing professional obligation.

The following is a summary of key characteristics of helping for action:

1. The helper uses listening and reflecting skills to *discover central problems* and assess the helpee's situation.
2. The helper assists the helpee to state problems in *behavioral terms* as goals to be achieved.
3. The helper and helpee agree on the *priority of problems* to be solved and acceptable levels of success.
4. The helper utilizes his or her *full range of skills* to work toward helpee goals.
5. Helpees show that they are *aware of the consequences* of each action alternative.
6. The process is *monitored* continuously. The helper and helpee agree on *evaluation* of progress and any *changes in strategy* to be instituted.
7. The helper and helpee plan the *transition* from learning coping skills to maintaining new behaviors in their natural setting without the helping relationship.
8. The helper and helpee decide if the *primary goal* and subgoals have been reached and if the helpee has learned the principles and steps of the personal problem-solving process.
9. The entire helping process is *evaluated* and *examined for learnings* to be applied in future helping relationships.

The action approach is well suited to two general kinds of helping—*problem solving,* and *changing* or adding specific behaviors. First, we will consider a decision-making and problem-solving model with related skills. Then, we will look at some skill clusters helpful in changing specific behaviors.

Problem Solving and Decision Making

A significant number of helpee concerns can be translated into problems to be solved or decisions to be made among two or more alternatives. Common life decisions such as, "What career should I plan for?" "What changes should I make in my life?" "Should I marry this person?" "Should I stay here or take this new job offer?" are suited to this problem-solving strategy of helping.

A second important helper consideration is how to teach helpees to solve their own problems. We are not helping them very much if we provide a temporary process for helpees to solve immediate problems, and then they continue to seek out helpers every time they face a new problem. One strategy for learning this process is direct instruction in problem-solving procedure. Another strategy is simulation—an artificial or game approach similar to the real life situation. The helpee can make choices and experience consequences vicariously without dire results. An example is the Career Game by Varenhorst (1969), which provides simulated decision-making conditions for helpees planning a career. A fictitious person making career choices is presented, and helpees work in teams deciding how that person will spend his or her time over eight years. Decisions are interdependent, and scoring is based on probability tables that reflect job, education, and marriage opportunities in American culture. Many decisions are involved, and the consequences are known immediately to the teams so the helpee players can learn the problem-solving process from early feedback.

The Problem-Solving Process

The steps below follow general problem-solving sequences and are applied to many problems, but most of the illustrations are in the area of educational and career planning, as exemplified by Brammer and Shostrom (1977) and Krumboltz and Sheppard (1969). To make the following procedures meaningful, relate them to a present problem in your life. Record the steps you are taking and comments on how each step contributed to your action plan. These general steps are:

1. Establish a *relationship* and get the helpee *involved.* Helpees must be interested in the process and have hope that they have the power to make decisions that will influence their lives profoundly.
2. State and clarify the *problem* and determine *goals.* This step is a special application of the goal-setting process described in the preceding section.
3. Determine and explore *alternatives* to the more apparent solutions.

4. Gather relevant *information*. This step may take the form of active seeking and reading by the helpee, statements of fact by the helper, simulation games, films, or tests.

5. Explore *implications* of information and *consequences* of the alternatives.

6. Clarify *values* that underlie personal choices. Helpees must know what they desire and the order in which they value those desires. Lead helpees to explore their interests, competencies, family circumstances, social expectations, and realities.

7. *Reexamine the goals,* alternative choices, risks, and consequences. A final check on understanding the information and implications is made before the final decision.

8. *Decide* on one of the alternatives and formulate a *plan* for, or course of action implementing, that decision.

9. *Generalize* the process to new life situations.

10. *Try out* the plan for implementing the decision with periodic *reevaluation* in light of new information and changing circumstances.

Most people, particularly young ones, have limited life experiences in making decisions and are generally unfamiliar with this rational process. Therefore, many helpees must be taught this process through problem-solving interviews, direct trial-and-error experiences, and through simulations, such as career games, marriage games, and war games. Young helpees often ask outright, "What shall I do?" "What course should I take?" "Should I try drugs?" "What career should I choose?" "What college should I apply to?" Instead of giving advice or opinions, it is preferable to say, "I can't tell you because I don't know what is best for you; but I can help you decide for yourself what to do. Would you like to learn how?" Abundant evidence in guidance studies shows that school-age youth make poor decisions about many areas of their lives. An illustrative decision-making program designed for students from grades seven through nine is described by Miller and Gelatt (1971). They have constructed a program that includes helping young students to: (1) identify critical decision points; (2) recognize and clarify personal values; (3) identify alternatives and create new ones; (4) seek, evaluate, and utilize information; (5) take risks; and (6) develop strategies for decision making.

Magoon (1969) describes a procedure for decision making with adults called "effective problem solving." It is a thirteen-part procedure for teaching college students with educational-vocational planning problems how to solve problems by themselves, at their own pace, under monitoring by a counselor. Magoon's method is another illustration of teaching the problem-solving process to helpees. His model and format are adaptable to many problem-solving situations where group and independent study approaches rather than individual counseling are indicated.

Decisions in the areas of interpersonal problems, such as sexual behavior involving previously learned response patterns, are more complicated. Solutions to these problems involve relearning methods as well as applying rational problem solving described above. Adult helpees who face difficult choices, such as what to do with rebellious children, dependent relatives, errant spouses, or changes of work locale, must be taught this same problem-solving process as a substitute for acting on impulses, stereotypes, or advice.

Skills Required in Problem Solving

Most problem-solving skills are combinations of those described in other contexts: problem identification, goal setting, informing, interpreting, diagnosing, and evaluating feedback. A skill called *force field analysis* can be applied to Step 3, generating and weighing alternatives. This skill utilizes physics concepts of fields of force and polarized valences, and is a method of comparing personal and social forces that are, at the same time, propelling and distracting helpees from their goals. Force field skills apply to many decision-making situations. The helpee's goal is stated briefly at the top of Figure 7, and the direction of solution is indicated by an arrow. The forces pushing him toward his alternative goal (in this simple illustration, to reduce weight by three pounds a week for six weeks) are indicated by a + sign, and those working against him by a − sign. After listing the + and − forces, a helpee can see more clearly where he is in relation to the feasibility of

FIGURE 7. ILLUSTRATION OF FORCE FIELD ANALYSIS

GOAL: Reducing Weight by Three Pounds a Week for Six Weeks. →

+	*Rank*		*Rank*
Spouse likes me thinner	1	Like rich food	3
Better for my health	2	Dislike diets and diet foods	1
Live longer	3	Lack knowledge of low calorie foods	2
Clothes will fit better	1	Will smoke instead of eat	2
Less fatigue	3	Three pounds seems too much in a week	1

↓ Balance point for forces

his goal. He then can rank the forces on their strength by rating each from 1 to 3, with 1 as the strongest rating. Now the helpee can decide on a strategy of strengthening the + forces or weakening the − forces. If it is a conflict of choice problem, each alternative goal can be analyzed and then compared. Drug counselors, for example, would find such a model useful when helping youth to decide whether to become involved with hard drugs.

The following list is a summary of problem-solving steps:

1. *Involve* the helpee.
2. State the *problem,* assess the *setting,* and determine the *goal.*
3. State and explore *alternatives.*
4. Gather *information.*
5. Explore *implications.*
6. Clarify *values.*
7. *Reexamine* goals, alternative choices, risks, and consequences.
8. *Decide* from alternatives.
9. *Generalize* to other situations.
10. *Evaluate* the process.

Behavior-Changing Skills

Modeling

Modeling is a method of learning by vicarious experience or imitation, such as watching the performance of others. The research evidence (Bandura 1969, Krumboltz and Thoreson 1976) suggests that a wide variety of behavior can be changed through modeling, and common sense experience attests to the power of examples also. Helpees tend to do what the helper does. If helpers use colorful street language to express themselves, so will the helpee; if helpers disclose personal data about themselves, the helpee will be more inclined to do so. One of the problems in helping interviews is that helpees do not know what to do, and verbal explanations often do not help. A helper who models expression of feeling gives the helpee a clearer picture of what behavior is expected. Another requirement is that the helper's behavior be at a higher level of functioning than the helpee's performance so the helpee has a behavioral model to strive for (Carkhuff 1969).

Role playing is another example of vicarious behavior where the helpee can see, through roles performed by others, what is expected. If she is fearful of approaching an employer about a job, for example, the helper can perform the role of an applicant (the helpee), as the helpee acts as the employer. The two then continue until the helpee sees other ways of acting in an employment interview. Then the helpee tries on the new behavior herself through reversing roles and having them critiqued repeatedly until she learns the new behavior to her satisfaction.

A third example of modeling effectiveness is the removal of fears by observing fearless behavior in a model, acquiring information about the feared object, and finally, having a direct experience with the threatening object with no ill effects. This approach would be effective with fears of snakes or of making speeches, for example.

Modeling seems to be most effective when the model has characteristics of status, competence, knowledge, and power. If the models possess qualities similar to helpers, they are effective. Advertising methods take advantage of these facts. Helpers thus need to discover which qualities are most attractive to helpees and then use them as guidelines for selecting models.

Modeling can be done by live, filmed, or taped methods. Although live methods have some advantages, such as maintenance of interest, filmed versions allow for more careful emphasis on the behaviors that one wants to model. An example of a helping situation with delinquent boys, which utilized live college-age models, is the work of Sarason (1968). Adolescent boys observed special modeling of the following situations: (1) vocational planning; (2) motivation and interests; (3) attitudes toward work and education; and (4) utility of socially appropriate behavior. When the boys observed socially acceptable models, they improved their own planning skills and ability to think in socially positive terms. The models were attractive to the boys, and role playing methods sustained their interest.

Filmed models have been used with effectiveness also. Hosford and Sorenson (1969) used audio tape and filmed models successfully with fourth to sixth graders who wanted to speak up more in class. Motivating teenage students to do the investigational work necessary to career planning is a problem also. Stewart (1969), using group models on audio tape, found that students improved their interest in career information and more actively explored sources of information after listening to the tapes.

General principles of using modeling are:

1. Determine which features of a model would be most *attractive* to the helpee.
2. Decide on the *objectives* of the modeling.

3. Choose *believable models* similar to the helpees in age, sex, and race.
4. Decide if *live or simulated modeling* would be more appropriate and practical.
5. Design a *modeling format,* script, or role-playing sequence.
6. Conduct the *modeling exercise.*
7. Discuss the *helpee's reactions* in terms of feelings, learnings, and suggestions.
8. Recognize that *informally we are modeling behaviors constantly* for helpees.

Rewarding Skills

At several points in this book we have described the reinforcing, or rewarding, effect of various helping procedures. This section will develop this idea as a consciously applied skill. The basic idea is that rewarded behavior tends to be repeated and that a wide variety of events can have reinforcing functions. We can use reinforcement to: (1) overcome behavior deficiencies (as in encouraging a helpee to plan ahead); (2) change undesirable behavior (as in eliminating chronic stealing); and (3) maintain present responses (as in encouraging statements of feeling).

Although the idea of using rewards to shape behavior is a simple one, there are some pitfalls. Most of the principles of reinforcement have come from learning studies in which animals were deprived of food and water, which then became the reinforcers. Since human responses are so much more complex, rewards have varied meanings. In helping situations we depend mainly on words, which have different effects depending on the cultural background of the helpee. Praise words, such as "good job," are used commonly, but soon lose their effect because of overuse, and because they have differing levels of potency for different people. Verbal rewards are most effective when the helper and helpee are working toward common goals. They are resented as blatant manipulation when used to influence helpees in ways that are not in their apparent best interests.

Some *general principles* in using reinforcement as a skill are that the reward, or incentive system, must be capable of maintaining a high level of action over a *long period.* In other words, the learning should be lasting. Secondly, the reward should depend on the presence of the behavior we want. But it is difficult to have the *desired behavior rewarded* consistently, because in ordinary life situations the reward is often badly timed or is given haphazardly. As a result, the undesired behavior is rewarded. Finally, the reward must be *strong* enough and given *often* enough for the desired behavior to be repeated. We also want the behavior to *generalize* to similar situations when the rewards are not present; for example, the helpee should be able to solve problems in other contexts. This reinforcement process is aided by using natural settings, varying the reward, and rewarding conditions systematically.

The *general strategy* for using rewards is to plan them selectively in a pattern so that the desired behavior is emitted in the form and sequence desired. This is a *reinforcement schedule* or *contingency*. We apply these stimuli (such as praise) in the appropriate strength and frequency until the appearance of the desired behavior is as strong and as frequent as required. With children, tangible reinforcers such as toys and candy are used. Adults respond to money, usually. The strategy begins with finding the *appropriate type* and *strength* of reinforcing agent.

Using tangible reinforcers is very controversial since some claim it to be similar to bribing. Bribery, however, is "pay" before the act whereas reinforcers are given after the act is performed. Nevertheless, it is generally conceded by writers on the subject (e.g., O'Leary et al. 1972) that social reinforcers, such as praise, are more desirable. Tangible reinforcers have a place if they are *not* used: (1) to *control* others; (2) to reward an act required in *daily living;* (3) to stop undesirable behavior (such as giving ice cream to stop crying); (4) to *replace* intrinsic rewards (such as self-satisfaction); (5) to *affect* others *adversely* (such as favoritism with rewards). Tangible reinforcers may be used to establish desired behavior, but they should be reduced as soon as possible. It is hoped that more *intrinsic* personal rewards will take their place and that people of all ages will outgrow their dependence on "gold stars." We must recognize, however, that people seemingly never outgrow their need for praise and affection, which usually remain through life as powerful reinforcers in the helping process.

Generally, it is desirable not to use "if statements" because they imply doubt about the person's willingness or ability to do the task. Instead of saying, "If you learn this vocabulary list, you can eat lunch," a preferred method is to say, "When you have learned this list, you can eat lunch."

A final word on strategy of reward is to *praise the action, not the person*. An example is, "I liked the way you helped Bob this morning, Jim," rather than, "You are a good boy, Jim, because of the way you help others."

The Achievement House proposal described in the previous chapter is an example of utilizing these principles of behavior modification.

Such a controlled environment makes especially effective use of rewarding skills.

This process may sound very mechanical and manipulative, but remember that we are describing a behavior change technique used in an ethical context where these methods are used with the helpee's knowledge and consent. If we are interested in the effects of these methods on the group, we can use these same principles at a social system level. Individual performance can be made contingent on the group performance and vice versa. We may design double reinforcement contingencies for the person and the group. For example, we can influence the degree of support, cohesiveness, productivity, and level of responsible behavior in individuals and groups by planning a suitable system of rewards.

Helping interviews or groups offer many opportunities to use rewards. If we want the helpee, for example, to focus on feeling expression, our attention to these expressions, as well as overt praise, will tend to increase this behavior. If initiative in seeking information to solve his problems is important, there are many ways to show approval in a reinforcing manner. This discussion of reward should make us more aware of all aspects of our helper behavior that have a reinforcing effect on the helpee's behavior.

Reinforcement has a decided effect on the helpee interview behavior, as demonstrated by Ryan and Krumboltz (1964). In decision-making interviews, they used verbal reinforcers such as "good" and "fine" and nonverbal reinforcers such as approval nods and were able to effect significant increases in helpee deliberation and decision responses. Similarly, a study of rural youth in group settings done by Meyer, Strowig, and Hosford (1970) revealed that information-seeking behavior can be increased considerably in eleventh graders by reinforcement methods. They found also that counselors could be taught to use these skills very quickly.

A summary of rewarding principles in the helping process follows:

1. *Reward performance,* not the person.
2. Determine the reward most *appropriate* to the helpee, considering unique interests, age, and setting.
3. Utilize *social* rather than tangible reinforcers.
4. Apply the reinforcer as *soon* after appearance of the desired behavior as possible.
5. As an *ethical* matter, obtain the understanding and permission of the helpee when using rewarding methods.

Contracting Skills

Contracting is a method for systematically arranging the rewards so that the probability of a response is increased. A contract is an agreement with the helpee that identifies the specific tasks both helper and helpee will perform in return for specific rewards. An example with a child helpee would be an agreement to get homework in regularly for one week in return for a special privilege. With an adult helpee an example would be the helpee's agreement to do some "homework" on a problem in return for helper talk time. Helping relationships with mature helpees have informal contracts that run something like, "I do (something specific) for you and in return you do (something specific) for me so we can achieve our mutual goals." Formal helping relationships, particularly forms labeled counseling and psychotherapy, are judged to be successful in terms of the extent to which both helper and helpee carry out their parts of the implied contract to reach certain goals.

Characteristics of contracts are: (1) *Specificity*—helpees know what is expected of them and the consequences for doing or not doing the agreed tasks. They make the choices so they learn to make decisions and to take responsibility for their own behavior. (2) *Impersonality*—the helpee is not emotionally obligated to do the agreed task, nor is the helper emotionally involved in the doing of the task. Both parties understand the consequences of not fulfilling the contract, so the whole issue of achievement is put on an impartial and impersonal basis. (3) *Feasibility*—the specified task must be in the behavioral repertoire of the helpee. If a helper expects the helpee to listen more accurately, the helpee must be able to attend for a sufficient time.

Although all helping relationships have implied contracts—understandings that both will have responsibilities to carry out—they usually are not formalized to the extent of writing down the conditions. Written contracts are constructed only when there is some doubt, as in the case of children, that they understand the nature of a "contract," or that they will respond with expected responsible behavior.

Formal contracts usually include statements of: (1) privileges extended; (2) responsibilities incurred; (3) bonuses and sanctions for completing or not completing agreed responsibilities; (4) how and by whom the contract is to be monitored. Contracts are commonly made between parents or teachers and children whose behavior has resulted in a breakdown of communication or confidence. Since these contracts are often "negotiated" with the help of an outside person, helpers should understand the principles and skills in behavior change contracting.

Some of the *conditions* to be determined before constructing the contract include: (1) identify the *specific behavior* that is *inappropriate;* (2) identify the *specific desired behavior;* (3) identify the *conditions* that *arouse* and *maintain* the inappropriate behavior (What sets off the behavior; what is the person *doing* at the time, and what are the *rewards* for doing it?); (4) collect *baseline data* about when the inappropriate behavior occurs; (How often? Who are significant persons to the helpee? Their influence?); (5) identify the *conditions* that *arouse* the *appropriate behavior* (What do the other persons do, or could they do, to arouse and reinforce this behavior?); (6) determine *reinforcers* and establish a *schedule* of reinforcement; (7) *negotiate a contract* with all persons concerned and *secure commitment* to it for a specified time.

Both informal and written contracts are used commonly in educational settings where specific tasks are to be performed. Homme's (1971) manual is a practical guide to writing contracts in a classroom, but it applies equally well to family situations where helpers often develop contingency contracts between parents and children and between husbands and wives. Conditions usually included in contracts are: (1) *Reward* should be given liberally, even for small approximations to the desired behavior. (2) Rewards, in small amounts, should be given *soon* after the performances. (3) Contracts should be *understood* clearly by all parties and be considered *fair* and reasonable. (4) The contract should be expressed in *positive terms,* such as "Finish your homework; then you can swim," rather than negatively, "Finish your homework or you will not get to swim."

A summary of principles for using contracting skills is:

1. Recognize a contract as an *agreement* between you and the helpee about the nature and conduct of your responsibilities.
2. Decide if a *formal contract* would facilitate the use of reinforcing conditions in a behavior change problem, or if an *informal agreement* would suffice.
3. Formulate the *contract* for the specified *time.*
4. Ascertain that all parties *understand* and *agree* to the contract.
5. Provide for *monitoring* the contract and deciding when the contract is to be *terminated.*

Extinguishing Skills

Extinguishing skills are closely related to reinforcing methods, since behavior gradually subsides and eventually disappears when rewards are discontinued. Thus, the skill element for the helper is applying extinction in systematic ways. If helpees want to change undesirable behaviors, for example, helpers assist them to identify the conditions that are reinforcing them and then to remove or weaken them.

Characteristics of extinction are that: (1) *rates* of extinction are *variable* and depend on the regularity of reinforcement, the effort required to perform, the perceived changes in the reinforcement pattern, and the availability of alternate responses; (2) *avoidance behaviors* can be extinguished by prevention of punishing consequences; (3) behavior is *displaced* rather than lost, since it can be reinstated quickly through reestablishing the reward schedule; (4) using extinction does *not guarantee* that more desirable behavior patterns will emerge.

Usually, after extinction of the undesirable behavior, efforts to elicit and reward desired behavior need to be undertaken. Behavior changes can be brought about most effectively by a *combination strategy* of extinguishing undesirable behavior along with modeling and reinforcing desirable behavior.

Methods of the extinction include: (1) simple *removal of reinforcing conditions* (as in not attending to an overly talkative helpee); and (2) gradually *changing the external stimulus* for an undesirable behavior, for example, by exposing the person in small increments to a fearsome situation, where the fear is minimally elicited and the fear response is blocked. Gradually, the fear will be neutralized. One method for doing this is through "behavior rehearsal," a kind of role playing (Lazarus 1966) in which helper and helpee role play scenes from actual problem situations. The method works well with helpees who want to be more assertive. In this case, the helper poses problems for the helpee around asking favors, making complaints, or refusing a request, in a gradual manner until the most difficult situations are encountered. The experience is critiqued, and occasionally the helper models the role of the helpee. The helpee is urged to try the new techniques under conditions where anxiety arousal is least probable. The advantage of this behavior-reversal method is that the helpee actively solves a close-to-life problem.

There are complex and still experimental methods for extinguishing avoidance behavior through massive exposure to highly noxious stimuli without injurious consequences. This process, known as *implosion* is not yet practical for most helpers. An example is helping a person to stop drinking by taking so much that he or she gets sick and avoids alcohol. Intensive imagery is used also to focus attention on unpleasant stimuli.

The main implication of extinction phenomena for helpers is to know how to change undesirable helpee behavior by removing the rewarding conditions. Does our intense attending behavior, for example, always reward the desired helpee behavior? Are there some behaviors, such as tendencies to overintellectualize, or to talk to the floor, that we would like to extinguish by altering the reinforcing stimuli? In summary, then, helpers can use extinction by showing helpees how they can remove rewarding conditions for unwanted behavior. They can help also by neutralizing undesirable emotional behaviors, such as fear of crowds, by gradually exposing helpees to fearsome situations or by helping them to avoid punishing consequences.

Aversive Control Skill

This skill, related to reinforcement and extinction, involves a process of removing undesired behaviors through use of "punishing" or "aversive" stimuli. The principal theory of aversive control is that the punishing effect results in a conditioned fear that has an inhibiting or suppressing effect. Aversive control is used to reduce undesirable and persistent responses that are self-reinforcing. Examples are self-punishing activities in children, and unwanted smoking, overeating, and drinking in adults. To be used successfully, however, aversive methods should be paired with a positive reinforcement program for desired behaviors. Usually, other forms of help are needed, since aversive control methods deprive helpees of much pleasure. They must be unusually cooperative and desire behavior change intensely.

Elements of aversive control are: (1) Introduce an aversive stimulus at the *time the person is engaging in the unwanted behavior.* Standard efforts for problem drinkers, for example, have been to put an emetic with their drinks so they get nauseous and vomit when they drink. Dire warnings of impending cancer are given to smokers when they light up. Temporary banishment from the group is effected for stealing property. (2) Develop a *positive reinforcing schedule for new behaviors* when the noxious behavior has ceased. (3) Be alert to *undesirable side effects* such as excessive fear arousal or unwanted negative attitudes toward the helper who suggested or administered the aversive stimulus.

Sometimes aversive consequences can be imagined with desirable effects. Helpees may be asked to fantasize situations like the ones they face. For example, a helpee may be having great trouble fighting with a demanding mother. He wants to avoid his strong responses, so with the aid of the helper, he imagines his demanding mother and works out alternative responses to her.

Desensitizing Skill

Desensitization is a method of reducing the emotional responsiveness to threatening or unpleasant stimuli by introducing an activity incompatible with the threat response. Sometimes this process is known as *counterconditioning.* For example, the helpee learns to associate fear of speaking up in class with an incompatible pleasant and relaxed feeling. The unpleasant response (fear) cannot be experienced when the pleasant response (relaxation) is present. Most desensitization activities are concerned with introducing relaxation in the imaginary presence of anxiety, although it has been used with feelings of anger and guilt also. Occasionally, desensitization is used in combination with modeling and reinforcement. (Appendix C includes a sample learning experience for the basic skill of desensitization.)

Desensitization methods were developed initially by Wolpe (1952) and were refined by him and numerous other behavioral scientists. There are several steps in desensitization procedure: (1) discussing conditions under which the problem occurs; (2) explaining the method and its rationale, as a learning process, to the helpee; (3) relaxation training; (4) constructing an anxiety hierarchy; (5) working through that hierarchy.

Steps 1 through 3 on defining problems and inducing relaxation were described in previous chapters. Step 4, hierarchy construction, is conducted at the same time as the relaxation training takes place. Essentially, the hierarchy is a list of 12 to 14 anxiety-producing situations around the same theme, such as taking tests. These situations are ranked in the helpee's imagination from lowest anxiety at the top to highest anxiety at the bottom. It is desirable to go over the list with the helpee to determine the strength of each and the equality of intervals between items. They should be evenly spaced as to their potency in arousing anxiety. In the fear of testing example, items would include initial events such as "waking up in the morning of the test" all the way to the test itself—"opening the cover page of the test booklet."

The items in the hierarchy should be similar to, or represent, the person's real life experiences. They should be sufficiently detailed to elicit a clear image of the incident. Items should include a broad sample of situations where the incident might take place. Helpees should be able to see themselves as actively involved rather than passively observing.

After the hierarchy is constructed and checked, the working-through process (Step 5) is begun. In the relaxed state helpees are asked to imagine a few neutral scenes, such as a path in the forest. Then they are asked to project themselves into the real problem and are given the top item in the hierarchy (lowest in anxiety). They are asked to indicate with a signal, such as raising an index finger, if they feel any anxiety. If so, relaxation exercises are undertaken again briefly. Then the helper returns to the hierarchy, reading the same item, and proceeding in the same manner through the hierarchy. If successful, helpees should still feel generally relaxed even after imagining the most potent anxiety provoking situation on their lists.

There are numerous nuances to the desensitization skill cluster. It is a sufficiently complex method to justify that you read more about it in the specialized readings at the end of this chapter and experience it yourself under an expert in the method. You can then try it yourself with a helpee under supervision until you master the steps.

The following list is a summary of desensitizing skill utilization:

1. Discuss *problem* with the helpee.
2. Decide if desensitization is *applicable.* (Desensitization might be indicated when a special isolated fear situation needs to be faced.)
3. Teach *relaxation* routines.
4. Construct *hierarchy* with the helpee.
5. *Test hierarchy* for rank order of *potency* and *evenness* of intervals between items by asking helpee, "Which is more anxiety provoking, A or B?"
6. Conduct *desensitization* by reading from the list, the least potent first, in about 30-minute sessions.
7. Check for relaxation and *repeat items* from the hierarchy until relaxed—stop and go back to relaxation methods if you cannot go on without anxiety.
8. Complete *entire hierarchy* (usually 12–20 items).

Expected Outcomes

You now have competencies to: (1) describe the behavioral approach to changing specific performance; (2) identify the principal steps in the problem-solving and decision-making sequences; (3) demonstrate that you can help a person through the steps in problem solving; (4) describe and illustrate behavior-changing skills of modeling, rewarding, contracting, extinguishing, aversion controlling, and desensitizing. Since the criteria of success with action skills are more apparent than with understanding and comfort skills, more clear outcomes can be observed. You can determine if your helpees did what they said they were going to do and to what level of proficiency.

Suggestions for Further Study

Bandura, A., *Principles of Behavior Modification.* New York: Holt, Rinehart & Winston, 1969. (General principles on which behavior changing methods can be built.)

———, "Psychotherapy and the learning process." *Psychological Bulletin* 58 (1961); 143–57. (Basic article on applications of learning principles to the helping function of psychotherapy.)

Brammer, L., and Shostrom, E., *Therapeutic Psychology: Fundamentals of Actualization Counseling and Psychotherapy,* 3rd ed. Englewood Cliffs, N.J.: Prentice-Hall, 1977. (Ch. 12, Counseling with Couples and Families; ch. 13, Counseling on Life Style, Careers, and Rehabilitation; Ch. 14, Counseling on Problems of Values.)

Buckley, N., and Walker, H., *Modifying Classroom Behavior.* Champaign, Ill.: Research Press, 1970. (A simplified approach to changing behavior in class settings.)

Carkhuff, R., *Helping and Human Relations.* New York: Holt, Rinehart & Winston, 1969. (The appendix of vol. 2 contains a clear account of the process of desensitization.)

Grossberg, J., "Behavioral therapy: A review." *Psychological Bulletin* 62 (1964); 73–88. (Overview of limitations and possibilities of behavior modification methods.)

Krumboltz, J., *Revolution in Counseling: Implications of Behavioral Science.* Boston: Houghton Mifflin, 1966. (Collection of papers on the application of behavior change methods to the counseling function.)

———, and Thoreson, C., *Counseling.* New York: Holt, Rinehart & Winston, 1976. (Papers on behavior modification principles and techniques.)

———, and Krumboltz, H., *Changing Children's Behavior.* Englewood Cliffs, N.J.: Prentice-Hall, 1972. (A manual of helping methods with children from a behavioral viewpoint.)

Osipow, S., and Walsh, W., *Behavior Change in Counseling: Readings and Cases.* New York: Appleton-Century-Crofts, 1970. (A collection of papers in issues and cases in behavior change.)

———, *Strategies in Counseling for Behavior Change.* New York: Appleton-Century-Crofts, 1970. (A theoretical and practical approach to behavior analysis and counseling strategy.)

Rhodes, W., "Psychological techniques and theory applied to behavior modification." *Exceptional Child* 28 (1962); 330–33. (Principles underlying behavior modification in clear practical terms.)

Tyler, L., *The Work of the Counselor.* 2nd ed. New York: Appleton-Century-Crofts, 1961. (An overview of planning and decision-making counseling.)

Wolpe, J., *The Practice of Behavior Therapy.* New York: Pergamon Press, 1969. (Detailed account of desensitization with illustrative cases.)

Woody, R., Behavior therapy and school psychology. *Journal of School Psychology* 4 (1966); 1–14. (Overview of behavior modification methods for school settings.)

Zifferblatt, S., *You Can Help Your Child Improve Study and Homework Behaviors.* Champaign, Ill.: Research Press, 1970. (A practical guide for improving school performance.)

SEVEN

Learning and Thinking About the Helping Process

The purposes of this chapter are to describe ways of thinking about the helping process and to present methods of learning helping skills. The helper functions as a whole person, not only as a skilled technician, while in contact with the helpee. Thinking is part of the helper 's personhood. At times helpers evaluate the helping process while they conduct it, but generally they think about and evaluate themselves, their helpees, and the helping process in private after the helping event.

Theory as a Guide

Theorizing refers to a rational rather than a feeling function. Helpers need a guiding theory to help them make sense of the complex helping process. Of course, people can help others in ways described in chapter 1 without a thought about theory, but if they are going to work systematically in a helping function, they need some "hooks" on which to hang their experiences and some frame of reference for gaining perspectives on their work and improving their services. The main value of theory, in my opinion, is to give direction to the action phase of helping. Theory is not necessary to establish a relationship, but it becomes crucial when deciding to assist helpees in behavior change.

For example, the helpee's statement, "I have a problem and I want help," usually translates into, "I am unhappy with the way things are; I want to change . . . ," or "I want to decide. . . ." My theory of helping explains how I see this process of change taking place and where the focus of effort needs to take place. As one's helping theory develops, one experiences increased awareness of the process and increased ability to explain one's views to others.

Outcomes You Can Expect

This chapter describes the need for a systematic way of thinking about helping and the principal ways other helpers have described their work. The outcomes you can expect from studying this chapter are to: (1) identify guidelines for thinking about your own theory of helping; (2) describe contributions of the major categories of current helping theory; (3) identify a style of learning best suited to you; (4) list twenty theoretical concepts and vocabulary terms from varied theories used to describe helping skills; and (5) describe four methods for learning helping skills.

Each helper must develop his or her own style and theory about helping because each person has had different life experiences and has different ways of looking at people. We may find others' assumptions similar to our own, but each helper must take responsibility for revamping them into his or her unique ideas and beliefs. Freud was not a Freudian, and Rogers was not a Rogerian; each was himself, and each built on the wisdom of the past. Admiring disciples of these men often gave their own explanations of the helping process a Freudian or Rogerian label.

Helpers build theory through three overlapping stages. First, they reflect on their own experiences. They become aware of their values, needs, communication style, and their impact on others. Second, they read widely about the experience of other practitioners who have tried to construct a systematic theory based on their observations. In this sense, theories are a sophisticated form of common sense. Finally, the helper forges the first two items together into a unique theory. If the theory is written down in a systematic manner, given a label, and attracts followers, the helper may even become the founder of another theory of helping!

There is no one preferred helping theory. Each approach to more formal counseling and psychotherapy has limitations and strengths for explaining the events in the helping process. We are a long way from a generally applicable theory of helpfulness. The data from research studies and observation of students in practice reveal the impressive effectiveness of numerous styles and approaches. Although helpees generally are fair judges of what is effective with them, their judgments are not the final answer either. Some helpees profess to be helped by tea leaf readers, magicians, and other "helpers" with mystical and extravagant claims.

A Personal Theory of Helpfulness

Constructing a Theory

Basically, a theory should be a rationale for what one does in the name of helping. It should include basic assumptions of how people learn and change their behavior. It should have some element of how personality is put together (structure), how it develops (growth), and how activity is generated (motivation). My own theory of helpfulness contains a *philosophical* dimension that includes my values and expected outcomes. It is a statement of the kind of person who should emerge from the helping process—an ideal growth model. Theory has a *structural* dimension that provides a cognitive map for looking at the person totally, and specifically at his or her current stage of growth. It is a scheme for helping to picture how the helpee's personality is organized. A *developmental* dimension is important to help differentiate the helpee's various normal and deviant growth stages as he or she moves from dependence to independence, from incompetence to competence, and from simplicity to complexity. Finally, a *process* dimension helps to explain how people learn and modify their behavior. Some persons need to experience something first and then reflect on the learnings—experiential learning. Others need to understand it and see all the parts first and then do it—cognitive learning. Occasionally, some use a trial-and-error process and seem to stumble into answers to problems, or insights emerge unexpectedly—discovery learning. Each of us has a style that works best under a given set of learning requirements, and our basic task in learning how to help others is to discover our most effective learning style.

As you think about your own theory of helpfulness, the following questions should be considered:

1. *Values and goals:* What is my view of the "good life"? What is my model of an effective, well-functioning, mature person for existing in our society at the present time? What do I want for this life? What is my responsibility to others?

2. *The nature of humanity:* How is the human personality structured? What motivates a person to behave as he or she does? How do thinking processes take place? What are the relationships among thinking, feeling, and valuing? How does a person make choices? Does each person create his or her own life, or does each live out the history of the race in an unique way?

3. *Behavior change:* How do we learn? Do we change the environment first, or our personality characteristics first, and then expect behavior to change? Do we act first, then learn; or do we obtain understanding first, then act? What does it mean to be helpful to another person?

These questions contain profound philosophical issues over which people have been arguing for centuries. Some are religious and require a declaration of faith; others are empirical and based on research. In any case, they illustrate the complexity, depth of thought, and length of time required to develop a comprehensive working theory about people and the helping process.

If you are ready to think through your own ideas about helping in a more formal way than in chapter 1, I suggest the following outline:

1. Know yourself—traits, values, beliefs about people on the dimensions listed above.
2. Read about what others have said about helping.
3. Write down the key ideas from your self-study and attractive features of others' views. Use a systematic form, such as: personal values and assumptions about people, main strategies and methods suggested by these assumptions, helping skills that are emphasized, and outcomes expected.
4. Finally, test the theory in practice and change it with experience. Our theory is also a guide to our practice, so that what we believe about the helping process influences the way we help others.

Usefulness and Limitations of Theory

A theory of helpfulness is useful when it enables one to describe and explain what one is doing in a helping relationship and why one is doing it. Theory is an intellectual tool to systematize and simplify the complex observations one makes continuously. It should help us fill in spaces in our perceptions that may be missing or vague, as we do when we put pieces in a puzzle. The process helps us in making choices of technique. If our theory focuses on rational problem solving, for example, we will utilize more rational methods, such as problem analysis, in our helping. If our theory stresses the significance of feelings, we will tend to focus on clarification of feeling states as a means to help.

If we have a theory with the elements described above, we should be better able to explain helpee behavior. If a helpee, for example, is exhibiting unusual avoidance behavior while making a choice among alternative solutions for a personal problem, we can guess about the person's fear of commitment or of risking failure. Our theory may give us informed hunches on why people resist choice or change. These hunches also serve as research leads that can be verified with more precise and extended observations, and through research.

The basic limitation of all theories, however, is that they are generalizations from observations of particular helping situations. When they are reapplied to an individual, one must be very careful not to oversimplify the situation or explain it away with a theoretical generalization. For example, our theory may indicate that generally the helper's self-revelation generates helpee self-revelation and that this is an essential condition to move the helping process forward. This generalization must be applied carefully to avoid destructive consequences of too much helpee self-revelation.

The principal value of the thinking process we have labeled theorizing is that helpers can *systematize* their observations so that they make sense to themselves and can be *communicated* to others. Theory is also useful when specific actions for the helpee must be outlined. Since each of the following theory groups espouses a different idea of how to get helpees to act and solve their problems, a helper needs to be familiar with the available options.

General Theories of the Helping Process

As described above, helpers tend to develop their own theories. For persons who operate rather intuitively, a simple statement of key assumptions may suffice. Others couch their theories in complex technical writings that at times seem mystical and even cultish.

Helpers who are visually or aurally oriented will use descriptive language to conform to their personal styles and language preferences.

Students and followers of past writers developed "schools" named after the person, such as Freudian, Sullivanian, or Rogerian. Descriptive titles, such psychoanalytic or behavioral, are used more frequently now. The following paragraphs list key features of the principal approaches currently in use. Such an outline has all the risks of oversimplification and biased selection, but the summaries are presented here as an orienting overview to classification, contributions, and limitations of helping theories. Detailed information about numerous specific theories may be obtained from the suggested readings section.

Eclectic

Most helpers have an eclectic orientation, taking a broad and flexible view on the critical questions about personality structure and behavior change. Although eclectic helpers synthesize concepts, techniques, and assumptions from many viewpoints, an eclectic view does not mean casual choosing from many different theories, a practice that has brought eclectic views into bad repute in some professional groups. It is a difficult theoretical stance to adopt because of the hard work required to integrate many complex ideas along a broad spectrum of helping functions; yet many established leaders among helping professionals are moving toward this integrative view.

Eclectic views must be consistent, as well as comprehensive. There appears to be renewed interest in a sophisticated eclecticism that emphasizes development of one's own personal theory of helping. It is still stylish in professional helping circles, however, to identify with a particular psychoanalytic, behavioral, or phenomenological view. This integrative viewpoint emphasizes use of all skill clusters included in Figure 2 of chapter 1, although each theory group emphasizes different skills at each stage in the helping process.

Psychoanalytic

The psychoanalytic view has a long history and perhaps the most complex set of assumptions and structures of all the helping theories. The essential idea is that understanding one's psychosexual life history and intrapsychic conflicts is crucial to working through personal problems and achieving normal development. Psychoanalytic writers following Freud, emphasized social learning as opposed to genetic influences in development. This view postulates a life energy that is stored in a location of the personality called the unconscious. The intrapsychic conflict among the various forms of energy expression in the person are the sources of human problems. Psychoanalytic theories are known as depth views because of their emphasis on life history factors and involvement of various levels of personality structure. The levels are ego (mastery), id (impulses), and superego (conscience). A key contribution of psychoanalytic theory to the helping professions is the idea of defense mechanisms whereby the personality seeks its internal stability by defending itself against disintegration within and attack from without. The principal means for helping people under this system is a process of working through their developmental problems into the present.

One of the main limitations of the psychoanalytic view is that, since their conflicts arise out of their past history, helpees consider their problems beyond their present control and responsibility. The methods of helping used in this approach are long, arduous, and unpredictable. Long and demanding training is required of helpers who wish to use psychoanalytic methods. The main skills emphasized by analytically oriented helpers are reflecting, confronting, interpreting, and informing.

Phenomenological

The phenomenological view of helping focuses on the uniqueness of each person's perception of reality. The helper is understanding to the extent that he or she can perceive the phenomenal world of helpees. The emphasis is on the present rather than the past or the future, and so how they feel about themselves and their worlds now is the crucial consideration. This view includes a cluster of theories, some of which emphasize a self as the main perceiving instrument. Sometimes these views are called *self-* or *client-centered* theories because they focus on persons and their perceptions of themselves. A key assumption is a person's drive toward growth and integration.

A related helping theory is *gestalt,* which emphasizes confrontation with self in the present. This view stresses honesty and openness in encounters with other people as the basis for helping and personal integration. Broadened awareness is one of the principal goals of gestalt helpers.

A cluster of phenomenological viewpoints known as *existentialism* is attractive to people helpers because of its focus on humanness. Existentialism is a philosophical outlook speaking to issues of time, meaning, purpose, feelings, and the human potential. The main skill clusters emphasized by this group are listening, reflecting, summarizing, and confronting (for understanding), with some supportive and centering skills (for awareness and comfort).

The main limitation of phenomenological and gestalt theories is their high degree of subjectivity, which leads to vagueness, mysticism, and problems of research.

Behavioral

Although most of the theories mentioned so far emphasize inferred subjective states such as feelings, the behaviorally focused helper concentrates on objective observation of behavior, especially on learning as a form of behavior change. In this sense all helping in formal counseling is behavioral, since learning or changing behavior in some form is the basic process. The main differences appear in explanations of how behavior changes and in the degree of emphasis put on outcomes in helpee behavior rather than on process. For the behavioral counselor the function of reward is very important because much evidence suggests that rewarded behavior tends to be repeated. If one wishes to increase the helpees' search for information to help them solve their planning problems, for example, helpers must see that their information-seeking behavior is rewarded in appropriate ways.

Behavioral helpers stress specific and concise goals, such as developing an educational plan or making a choice between two potential marriage partners. The main standard of success for such helpers is the degree to which their helpees reach their stated goals. This emphasis on precise goals and measurable outcomes is an attractive feature to helpers with a behavioral set. Because observable behaviors are the variables studied, the behavioral framework lends itself to research or counseling processes and outcomes. The principal skill clusters emphasized by this group are problem solving and behavior changing (for positive action). Principal limitations of behavioral views are the difficulties in dealing with feelings through observable behavior. The emphasis on specificity, precision, and objectivity tends to lead the helper to focus on minute pieces of behavior and to ignore larger complex patterns.

Empirical-Rational

Related to the behavioral approach is a cluster of viewpoints stressing *rationality*. Thinking processes are examined therein and corrected by pointing out faulty logic and assumptions to helpees on the assumption that altering their belief systems leads to changes in their behavior. Helpers using this approach would tell their helpees that their difficulties in making choices, for example, seemed to be due largely to their catastrophic expectations. Seeing clearly how their thinking was distorted would remove this obstacle to positive action. A teaching role, therefore, is one of the principal helping functions.

A large group of helpee problems revolve around making plans and choices that require information about one's self or the world of reality, like work. Educational-vocational planning of youth is an example. Here the emphasis is on rational *problem solving* and prediction of success in a given training event. Sometimes this viewpoint is known as the *trait and factor* theory because the focus of effort is assessment of personal traits and intellectual factors. This task of assessment is accomplished mainly through psychological tests that can predict success in study or work. Helpers stressing this viewpoint do not deny the significance of feelings in human events, but they tend mainly to focus on the more observable rational events in the helping process. Computer technology is being tapped as an adjunct to the helping process where information and prediction are special needs. The main skill clusters emphasized by this group are confronting, interpreting, and problem solving. The chief limitation of rational approaches is a disproportionate emphasis on rational and observable behaviors to the detriment of the vast feeling realm of existence.

Transactional-Communicative-Reality

The group of transactional-communicative-reality theories focuses on communication patterns among the interested parties, such as parent and child, or teacher and pupil. A study is made of the interactional patterns and the mechanisms people use to influence, manipulate, and reach other people. The assumption is made that all of us carry within ourselves remnants of child, parent, and adult communication patterns. The helping process consists of examining these patterns, in particular, the distortions of these states of being between individuals (transactional analysis). One form of distortion, for example, is the "game" helpees play with themselves and others. Helping is facilitated by training in communication skills so that intentions are matched with behaviors. Feelings, as well as thought patterns, are considered. Much responsibility is placed on helpees for their own choices and actions. Helpees are taught that they are responsible for their own behavior, meaning that they must "own" their own problems rather than blame others. This theoretical framework is used extensively with family problems where communication patterns are complex, rigid, and distorted. The main skill clusters emphasized are listening, reflecting, confronting, and interpreting (for increased awareness and understanding). The principal limitation of this cluster of communication approaches is its limited set of assumptions about behavior; a more comprehensive view usually is required to deal with the complexities of family problems.

Physiological

Although there is no general physiological category among helping theories, there is a strong emphasis in helping interviews and groups on body awareness, sensory awakening, and brain wave functions. The basic idea is that many of our difficulties in living effectively result from our losing touch with the physical dimension of our existence. We deny our impulses, dilute our sensory awareness, and ignore messages from our bodies. Helping effort is devoted to enriching life through reawakening the senses, opening awareness to our bodies, enjoying physiological processes, and utilizing knowledge of alpha brain waves to promote relaxation and self-understanding. Methods used are relaxation, breath control, fantasy, massage, touch, and feedback control of brain waves. This training is conducted through growth centers such as Esalen Institute. In the United States alone there are over 130 such growth centers. The main skill clusters emphasized by this group are confronting, interpreting, and supporting.

Teaching and Learning Basic Helping Skills

There are two important reasons for studying this topic of training. Many helpers are asked to train others in workshops, staff development programs, and adult education courses. In addition, it is a well-established principle (Carkhuff and Berenson 1967) that an effective helping strategy with individuals is to perceive helping as teaching helpees basic life skills so they can solve their own problems.

A second reason for studying this topic is that students of helping skills have their own best learning styles. Some, for example, learn skills best by seeing a demonstration or a model film of the skill; others want to read about the skill and understand the rationale and steps before practicing it. Some want to try the skill in role-playing, hence less risky, experiences. Still others learn most effectively by experiencing a helping relationship with little preparation; then they see a video tape and receive feedback on their performance. This is known as the experiential approach.

There are three basic strategies for learning helping skills—skills practice, experiential learning, and didactic knowledge. Knowing about these differences in teaching-learning style will enhance your awareness of various helping skills and your understanding of the preceding chapters. But simply reading about them probably will not improve your skills much. You need practice under the strategy best suited to you, and then you need feedback on your performance of the helping skills.

Part and Whole Approaches

Microskills Methods

The skills presented in the preceding chapters have been demonstrated to be effective through research or practice. A basic method for learning these precise skills is called microskills training, an instructional strategy that divides a large category of skills into simple teachable behavioral components. These skills then can be combined into numerous interview combinations.

An advantage of the microskills approach is that the instructor can be specific about describing helping skills, rather than using general suggestions such as "Listen to your helpees!" The microskills are so basic to effective communication that they fit easily into every theoretical framework or helper setting. Effective helpers use these skills, not as mechanically applied formulas for helping, but as a repertoire of basic communication skills.

It is paradoxical that the main limitation of the microskills approach is its specificity. Integrating the components of complex helping skills into a smooth helping process is not easy. It is like teaching swimming by training people to use their arms, hands, legs, and breathing apparatus separately—and then telling them "Now you are swimmers." How can they then combine these component skills into the beautifully coordinated act we call swimming? Such analysis seems artificial, but experience in counselor education shows that students can become so involved in skills practice that they perceive them not as techniques but as natural manifestations of good human relations and effective interpersonal communications.

A microskills approach provides you with considerable flexibility of choice. The microskills teaching approach seems the best compromise between a strategy of teaching general principles, which assumes transfer of those principles to skills, and the precise "cookbook" approach that attempts to tell you what to do and how to do it under specific circumstances. It is important to maintain a broad perspective on the whole helping process (the polished swimmer), as well as to attend to the fundamental skills. The challenge is to produce a smoothly integrated champion from careful attention to fundamentals without making those fundamentals the exclusive focus.

Chapter 1 stressed the importance of fundamental component skills training, combined with helper self-understanding and broad awareness of the total helping task, as the most effective preparation for the helping function. Seeing appropriate and inappropriate models, along with understanding the ideas and purposes behind the skill, makes the learning process even more effective. Practicing the skill and receiving feedback on the tryout performances are essential elements also. Repeating performances until the desired level of skill is achieved constitutes the final phase of this model.

Ivey (1977) used a training model in his study of microcounseling, for example, that contained the following steps: (1) a five-minute taped interview to establish a natural baseline measure of the trainees' interviewing behavior; (2) reading a description of the technique; (3) viewing video tape models of effective and ineffective use of skills; (4) viewing the initial baseline tape noting specific instances of using the new skill effectively and ineffectively; (5) discussing the skill procedures with a supervisor or colleague; (6) completing another five-minute taped interview sample with the same helpee, thus giving the trainee an opportunity to demonstrate his or her skill; (7) repeating the cycle until the desired level of competence is achieved. The success of this method hinges to a large extent on the adequacy of the supervisory relationship. It is thus difficult to learn helping skills by independent study alone.

The key to improvement in the microcounseling skills approach is immediate feedback on performance. The new skill is practiced until the desired performance standard is met. Truax and Carkhuff (1967) utilized a similar program integrating the teaching of concepts and experiencing feedback on actual performance of basic skills. Gordon (1970) developed a skills package designed for small groups of parents or teachers who want to practice more effective ways of communicating with children. Kagan (1971) has packaged a program on "influencing human interaction" that has filmed models, skill practice units, and feedback systems called "interpersonal process recall." This is a method of video taping a short interview with a helpee. An independent interviewer talks with the helpee immediately afterward about his or her reactions to the experience, while the helper watches the inquiry interview. Then the helper is interviewed similarly. Finally, both come together with the person conducting the inquiry interviews and the observers to discuss their reactions to the original helping interview and to make recommendations for improving skills and process.

Others who have published experimental programs involving media, readings, and exercises in basic human interaction skills are Danish (1971), Kagan (1971), and Jung (1971). Cunningham (1970) has created a packaged program for increasing competencies of practicing counselors. Appendix A of this book includes samples of brief skills practice exercise guides that I have used in training programs.

The programs cited above are examples of bridging the gap between theory and practice. They are not established do-it-yourself programs but experimental systems designed to help groups master basic human interaction skills with minimal expert instructional leadership.

Simulations. The best known example of this learning strategy, related to microcounseling, is role playing. The trainee takes the role of a helpee and tries to become that person as much as possible. Although the actual problem is artificial, the simulated helpee tries to make it as real as possible, even to taking a problem from his own experience.

The helper then simulates the helper role, continuing for about ten minutes, or until enough time has passed for adequate practice of the basic skill. This can be done as a demonstration and discussion stimulator in front of a group or in helping trios.

A variation on the role playing method is to ask three persons to leave the room while the group develops a helpee role and asks one of the group to simulate the helpee. Then the absent "helpers" are brought in one at a time to do their helping sequences with the simulated helpee. One advantage of this method is that the group can compare several styles of helping, and the feedback from the simulated "helpee" to the interviewers is most often a powerful educational experience for all. This technique can be extended into more complex dramatic situations where classrooms, families, and meetings are simulated and acted out with props, scenes, and directors. An advanced form of this simulation is known as "psychodrama."

Occasionally coached helpees or even professional actors have been utilized to provide simulated helping conditions close to real problems. Kagan (1971) has used video taped actors presenting different human problems in short clips. Helper trainees are then asked to make responses as if this were an interview. They imagine they are alone with the person on the screen.

A useful teaching method for basic skills is the "round robin helping trio" in which three people who are learning the skills together practice and give each other feedback on their performance. One is a simulated helpee, another the helper, and the third an observer of the process. After a brief skills practice sequence they stop and discuss the experience, including the observer's comments. Then, the whole process is repeated two more times with trio members changing roles. This process is illustrated in figure 8.

A whole array of "games" has been constructed to deal with real life problems in simulated form. There are "career," "war," "ghetto," and "marriage" games. These games allow intense involvement without the risks and complexities of real life situations. At the same time they provide sufficient data when properly conducted to generate very productive learnings about self and interpersonal relationships. Although these are not direct helping simulation devices, they provide awareness for helpers on how they react in conflict, prejudice, crisis, problem-solving, and decision-making settings.

Experiential Learning

Beginning with a real experience is the key feature. Experiential learning involves doing the actual task and then discussing the experience and learning derived. It is known as the "do-look-learn" ap-

FIGURE 8. ROUND ROBIN HELPING TRIO

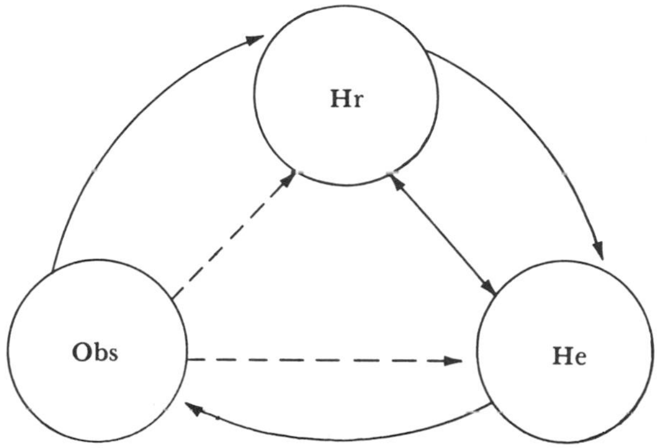

proach. The helper, for example, actually interviews a person seeking help; then the helper and helpee describe how they felt about the experience and what they did. The observers, if there are some, offer their emotional and cognitive reactions. Then, the principals and the observer group discuss what they *learned* from the experience—about helping skills, communication skills, or listening methods.

The values of experiential learning are very great, but it has some limitations. It is a high risk activity for helpers because they take the great leap into the experience without knowing the consequences. Sometimes they end the experience in a heap of frustration and humiliation or, at worst, with no feelings. Occasionally they feel the exhilaration flowing from discovery of new resources and skills not hitherto realized. Such learning has some risks for the helpee too, because the helping encounter usually is not a simulated situation but a real plea for help. There is an ethical question about assigning a naive student helper to a helpee struggling with real problems. In formal training settings this issue is resolved somewhat by the usual presence of an experienced supervisor and fellow trainees who provide support as well as critical feedback on training performance.

Various growth groups designed to provide helper trainees with self-awareness and skills practice fall in this experiential learning category. Here, the trainees arrange themselves in a group and interact at increasingly more trusting and close interpersonal levels. Learning outcomes flow from the frequent efforts of the leader, or learning facilitator, to stop the action and to look at both the learning process they are going through and what is happening to them as individuals. During the group process itself, however, members are constantly giving and receiving feedback to their helping skills. Some instructors of basic helping skills lean almost entirely on this experiential form of learning through groups to provide the kind of self-awareness and skills training required of helpers.

A variation on experiential learning common among early helping professionals was the "didactic analysis." This method of learning therapy by going through an analysis experience oneself is still utilized in psychoanalysis. Counselors and psychotherapists often learn the principles and skills of the helping process in a similar manner, but it is a costly, one-to-one tutorial method of skill learning.

The traditional didactic strategy of teaching general principles and knowledge has little efficacy when used alone. When combined with skills training and experiential learning, however, behavioral science fact and theory have their place in a helper program. They provide a basis for judgment and a framework for organizing experiences, such as the case made for theory in this chapter.

A Combined Strategy Approach

The learning system I prefer, and that I see as having much support in research and practice, combines the microskills, experiential learning, and didactic strategies. My approach is roughly as follows: (1) practice microskills in a simulated laboratory setting with constant critiques; (2) expose one's self to intensive self-awareness experiences (usually along with (1); (3) put skills together into appropriate patterns in a practicum setting with real helpees and close supervision; (4) practice skills in natural helping relationships in agencies, at home, and with friends. Special knowledge and skill inputs such as theory, research methods, and referral resources are acquired as needed through conventional classes, independent study, or tutorials.

With the current emphasis on experiential learning there appears to be growing skepticism about the value of direct teaching of helper characteristics, such as sensitivity to feelings of helpees. The old assumptions about automatic transfer from lectures on "how to do it" to actual practice are not valid, but forms of programmed instruction may be useful as supplements to other methods. Bullmer (1972), for example, studied the acquisition of interpersonal perceptual skill through a programmed self-instructional method. He demonstrated that effective person perceivers can be "made" through knowledge of concepts related to interpersonal perception, sources of error in perception, identifying feelings, and identifying hidden meaning. The learner then practices applying this knowledge through examples. The basic issue again is, how can you as a learner make the best use of the three basic strategy principles—experiential, skills training, and didactic knowledge?

In summary, it is essential to have practice in basic skills (through exercises and simulations), opportunities for self-awareness (through counseling and group experience), and exposure to real life problems and helping relationships to put the whole process together. While it appears to be a safe assumption that some of the learnings acquired in laboratory settings and independent reading do transfer to helping relationships, there is no substitute for direct self-initiated experience with immediate feedback on performance from specialists and peers.

Basic Theory Underlying Skills Application

Four theoretical threads run through the skills described and illustrated earlier. Concepts from theories based on needs, learning, awareness, and communications will be used.

Needs

The first theoretical thread is the *need approach* to motivation described in chapter 1. Human beings are energized by basic psychological and physiological needs that push for satisfaction and stabilization of the personality, but occasionally they seek risky behavior to provide variety. That people act to satisfy their needs is the basic idea of this viewpoint. Helping skills are designed to assist helpees to fulfill their needs for understanding, comfort, and action.

Learning

A second thread tying the helping skills together is a behavior change, or learning, approach. A key concept useful for skill development is *modeling,* the use of examples of effective and ineffective helping skills. *Reinforcement,* or management of rewards, is another key learning concept. Rewarded behaviors tend to become fixed in the repertoire of the person; satisfying a need tends to be a reinforcing condition, for example. Conversely, behaviors that are not rewarded, such as those that are ignored or that may even be aversive or noxious, tend to disappear from the behavioral repertoire of the person. The principle of *transfer* is important for skill learning also, since the skills learned in simulated, or artificial gaming, settings are transferred to similar real life helping situations. Practicing listening skills in a controlled laboratory setting, for example, can then be applied in comparable helping interviews. *Stimulus substitution,* or reconditioning, also takes place in some helping situations. We may wish to substitute a relaxation response, for example, for a tension response in a test situation. *Goal setting* and *problem solving* are important in the learning approach also.

Awareness

A third theory covers the idea of *awareness of feelings* and their effects. As indicated earlier in this chapter, our reality is what we perceive it to be. Therefore, when we talk about understanding, we mean perceiving the helpee's unique way of looking at the world. The helper responds to helpees in such a way that they perceive themselves as being understood. Helpees manifest this understanding by verbal behavior that describes their subjective feelings, such as "I feel confident," or "I feel angry toward you," or "I feel good about you and me," or "Now I know where it's at."

Communications

A fourth thread that ties the whole skill bundle together is *communications* theory. An underlying assumption in helping is that people do not understand one another because they cannot communicate with one another. Therefore, skills covered in earlier chapters are aimed at facilitating interpersonal communication by listening and speaking more clearly. The basic communications problem is to make one's intent as a speaker clear by matching intent with words. The result is directness and clarity of meaning. Bandler and Grinder (1975) speak of "denominalization" as a basic helping function of clarifying helpee sentences.

The usual state of affairs, however, is a communications gap where the effect on the hearer does not match the message the speaker intended, and so much time is spent in clearing up the resulting misunderstanding. Sometimes this condition is caused by a double message—one given by one's body, which says "I'm afraid," and another by one's words, which say "I'm calm and confident." The result is confusion in the hearer and projection of personal meanings on the mixed message.

It seems almost absurdly simple to state that often the most helpful thing we can do is to make it possible for helpees to improve their communication. This approach includes attention to nonverbal, or body, language as well as speech. Our actions, rather than our words, are more honest and direct forms of communication because we have learned that words can conceal, distort, and deny real feelings, but our bodies do not. As one helper, Perls (1969), expressed it clearly, "Our bodies do not lie." One means to make our messages more clear, then, is to get in touch with our bodies (our feelings) so we know what they are saying. By pointing out discrepancies between verbal messages and body messages in helpees, we help them to communicate more consistently and clearly with themselves and others.

The preceding discussion implies that communication problems in helping interviews result from unclear intent of, or confused messages from, helpees. We need to remind ourselves constantly that communication, a two-way process, requires that we look into the way we distort what we hear from helpees. Are my needs, of which I am unaware, acting as "filters" through which I hear the helpee's message my way? If I am only vaguely aware, or creating fantasies about this helpee, do I hear what I *want* to hear? Am I fearful that I will be attacked, seduced, or "conned"? Am I fearful that I might do the same to the helpee? The kinds of awareness and the conditions discussed in the earlier chapters under transference and countertransference and cultural bias help here. The main point is that unrecognized needs and feelings distort messages and compound problems.

Expected Outcomes

The major outcomes you should have achieved by studying this chapter are: (1) you have thought through your own ideas about helping and have the beginnings of your own unique theory; (2) you have a basis for improved judgment about the use of theory and research flowing from theory to affect your helpee's behavior constructively.

As a result of studying methods of learning helping skills you can: (1) identify a style of skill learning best suited to you; (2) plan the next steps for improving your helping skills; (3) select a learning method to develop your skills; (4) describe your learning tasks and outcomes with concepts and vocabulary from various theories of helping.

Personal Epilogue

This brief venture into the nature of the helping process and related skills has been like a conversation with you. At times I found myself persuading you to accept my point of view, and at other times, confronting you with a challenge to examine your beliefs about people and your style of helping. I did not intend to present an exhaustive formal treatise on the philosophical and scientific bases of helping. Rather, this book has been a distillation of my experiences with helpees, a composite of my dialogues with colleagues and students, and a summary of my readings through the vast literature on helping. It is my hope that these ideas will assist you to tap your resources, provide a framework for thinking through your experiences, and offer methods for improving your helping skills.

Helping relationships and behavior technology present a monumental challenge and opportunity to all people to make this world a more human place to live. We need to remind ourselves constantly that the main objective of all helping activity is self-help—teaching people the skills they need to work out their own problems and achieve their own growth goals. I am convinced from personal experience and observation that we must seek constantly for more effective helping modes and methods. We begin this process, I believe, with rigorous self-renewal followed by a continuous program of personal and professional growth. Evidence is mounting that our helping skills have little impact unless we are open to change, willing to risk, and are concerned about human welfare. The fact that helpees move toward their helper's interpersonal functioning level places a heavy burden on all helpers to be the best possible models of effective human beings.

Suggestions for Further Study of Helping Theory

Brammer, L., "Counseling Theory." *Encyclopedia of Education.* New York: Macmillan, 1971. (Ideas for developing a helping theory.)

———, and Shostrom, E., *Therapeutic Psychology: An Approach to Actualization Counseling and Psychotherapy.* 3rd ed. Englewood Cliffs, N.J.: Prentice-Hall, 1977. (Ch. 2 on overview of theories, their contributions and limitations; ch. 3 on a creative synthesis.)

Ford, D., and Urban, H., *Systems of Psychotherapy.* New York: John Wiley & Sons, 1963. (Detailed analyses and critiques of the major approaches.)

Harris, T., *I'm OK; You're OK.* New York: Harper & Row, 1969. (Popular version of transactional analysis terms and methods.)

James, M., and Jongward, D., *Born to Win.* Reading, Mass.: Addison-Wesley, 1971. (Application of gestalt theory and method.)

Krumboltz, J., "Behavioral Counseling. Rationale and Research." In *Behavior Change in Counseling: Readings and Cases,* edited by S. Osipow and W. Walsh. New York: Appleton-Century-Crofts, 1970. (Overview of behavioral approach to helping.)

Patterson, C., *Theories of Counseling and Psychotherapy.* New York: Harper & Row, 1966. (Detailed survey of major writers on helping theories.)

Rogers, C., *Client-Centered Therapy.* Boston: Houghton Mifflin, 1942. (Description of client centered and phenomenological views.)

Stefflre, B., ed., *Theories of Counseling.* New York: McGraw-Hill, 1965. (A series of papers by different authors on the major theories of counseling.)

Suggestions for Further Study of Learning How to Be Helpful

Bigge, M., *Learning Theory for Teachers.* New York: Harper & Row, 1964. (An elementary description of the principal theories of learning.)

BILODEAU, E., ed., *Principles of Skill Acquisition.* New York: Academic Press, 1969. (A collection of papers on skills from a systems viewpoint.)

BOOCOCK, S., ed., *Simulation Games in Learning.* Beverly Hills, Ca.: Sage Publications, 1968. (A manual on the theory and practice of games as learning aids.)

BRADFORD, L., BENNE, K., and GIBB, J., *T-Group Theory and Laboratory Method.* New York: John Wiley & Sons, 1964. (An elaboration of the laboratory method and use of T-groups.)

BROWN, G., *Human Teaching for Human Learning.* New York: Viking Press, 1971. (An introduction to confluent education—the integration of cognitive and affective education.)

BRUNER, J., *Toward a Theory of Instruction.* Cambridge, Mass.: Belknap Press, 1966. (How to use research knowledge in forming one's views of the learning process.)

BUGELSKI, B., *The Psychology of Learning Applied to Teaching.* Indianapolis: Bobbs-Merrill, 1971. (How to develop a theory and strategy of learning and instruction.)

CARLSON, E., *Learning through Games: A New Approach to Problem Solving.* Washington, D.C.: Public Affairs Press, 1969. (Learning to solve problems through simulated situations.)

CHESTER, M., *Role Playing Methods in the Classroom.* Chicago: Science Research Associates, 1966. (An introductory approach to role playing teaching methods.)

IVEY, A., *Microcounseling: Interviewing Skills Manual.* 2nd ed. Springfield, Ill.: C. C Thomas, 1977. (Suggestions and illustrations for learning microcounseling skills.)

———, and GLUCKSTERN, N., *Basic Attending Skills* (1978) and *Basic Influencing Skills* (1976). Amherst, Mass.: Microtraining Associates. (Leader and participant manuals and illustrative video tapes for teaching basic helping skills.)

KAGAN, N., *Interpersonal Process Recall: A Method of Influencing Human Interaction.* Washington, D.C.: American Personnel and Guidance Association, 1976. (A system with guidelines and films to learn interaction skills through use of a feedback system called "interpersonal process recall.")

ROGERS, C., *Freedom to Learn.* Columbus, Ohio: Charles E. Merrill, 1969. (An elaboration on experiential learning.)

ZUCKERMAN, D., and HORN, R., *The Guide to Simulation Games for Education and Training.* Cambridge: Information Resources, 1970. (A practical list of games both experimental and marketed.)

A

Exercise for Learning Attending Behavior

Introduction to Appendices

The following appendices are included as examples of brief skill exercise outlines. These outlines include the essential elements in a learning exercise: (1) audience intended; (2) concept or skill to be learned; (3) purpose of the exercise; (4) learning objectives; (5) learning activities; and (6) evaluation. The outlines are included as illustrations of skill exercises you can construct for yourself, not as do-it-yourself exercises to be followed verbatim.

Audience:

Students of helping procedures.

Concept:

Attending behavior is the helper's attempt to focus on the helpee communication through nonverbal means, such as eye contact, gestures, and postures, and selected verbal responses that indicate the helper is in contact with the helpee.

PURPOSES:

1. To communicate interest in the helpee.
2. To communicate understanding of what the helpee is saying.
3. To reinforce relationship interactions.

LEARNING OBJECTIVES:

1. To demonstrate attending behaviors in a microskills learning setting (eye contact, gestures, posture, verbal response) such that helpees report satisfactory helper interest in them and understanding of their statements.
2. To demonstrate attending behaviors in other interaction settings, in and out of class. These behaviors are natural and effective as indicated by feedback from fellow learners.

LEARNING ACTIVITIES:

1. Verify understanding of the concept after brief explanation.
2. View demonstration of attending behaviors.
3. View models of attending behavior in a helping process on video tape.
4. Practice skills in a round robin simulation structure.
5. Debrief exercise in trios.
6. Debrief exercise with total group.

EVALUATION:

1. Learners obtain feedback from simulated microskills learning exercise regarding effectiveness of their attending behaviors. Learners continue skills practice until this observer and simulated helpee report satisfactory attending behaviors.
2. Learners report to their trios on feedback regarding effectiveness of attending behaviors in everyday human interactions and helpee relationships.

B

EXERCISE FOR LEARNING PARAPHRASING SKILLS

AUDIENCE:

Students of helping procedures.

CONCEPT:

Paraphrasing is a basic component of listening skill indicating the helper's understanding of the helpee's intent and messages. Paraphrasing is a method of stating the helper's understanding of the helpee's message in order to test that understanding.

PURPOSES:

1. To increase the accuracy of communication through aiding the helper to translate helpee language responses from less to more familiar, obscure to more clear and precise, and from complex to more simple forms.
2. To operationalize, in part, what it means to understand a helpee and to communicate that understanding.

Learning Objectives:

1. To paraphrase helpee statements accurately such that they agree in this exercise with three out of four attempts.
2. To use this skill in all human relationships as manifested by consistent efforts to paraphrase a speaker's meaning.

Learning Activities:

1. Read John Wallen's paper "Paraphrase: A Basic Communication Skill for Improving Interpersonal Relationships."
2. Verify understanding of the concept and the method.
3. View demonstration of paraphrasing methods.
4. Practice skills in trio round robin structure.
5. Debrief exercises in trios.
6. Debrief exercise with total group.

Evaluation:

1. Learners obtain feedback regarding achievement of skill to level cited in objective 1 above.
2. Learners report to their trios later on their use of paraphrasing skill in everyday personal and client relationships.

C

Exercise for Learning Desensitization Skills

Audience:

Students of helping procedures.

Concept:

Desensitization is a process of reducing anxious behavior by substituting a response that inhibits the anxiety. Stimuli that evoke anxiety are presented in increasingly stronger forms to the point where anxiety is no longer elicited. Anxiety is regarded as a learned response.

Purposes:

1. To reduce the helpee's discomforting anxiety in responses to specific real life stimuli.
2. To teach helpees how to control and reduce their anxiety without the presence of a helper.

Learning Objectives:

1. To understand the components of hierarchy construction, relaxation procedure, and hierarchy presentation.

2. To assist helpees to reduce their anxiety below the discomfort or dysfunction level by desensitization methods.

3. To be able to teach helpees to use desensitization methods without additional help.

Learning Activities (Through Dyads):

1. Construct anxiety response hierarchy (may be done as homework).

2. Review potency levels with the helpee (by asking "Is this item more disturbing than that one?"). Ascertain helpee's cooperation level, and continue only if helpee is cooperative.

3. Use relaxation exercise (standard progressive methods or a tape).

4. Present hierarchy items with lowest potency first; pause to let helpees fantasize on the item. Explain to them that they will try to replace their anxiety with feelings of relaxation. They should tell the helper by lifting their fingers if any of the items still make them anxious.

5. Repeat the relaxation exercise as necessary. Repeat the same item or go on to the next hierarchy item as indicated by the helpees' ability to reduce their anxiety. They may be instructed to practice this method at home for a half hour a day.

6. Each hierarchy item is presented in the manner of 4 and 5 until all can be fantasized without evidence of anxiety. When anxiety shows in response to an item the fantasy is stopped and the relaxation exercise is repeated.

Evaluation:

1. The exercise is completed when the helpees work through their hierarchies with anxiety below the discomfort or dysfunction level.

2. The method is regarded as successful when helpees can apply this method to their other real life situations.

Bibliography

Aguilera, D., and Messick, J. 1974. *Crisis Intervention: Theory and Methodology.* 2nd ed. St. Louis: C. V. Mosby.

Authier, J., Gustafson, K., Guerney, B., and Kasdorf, J. 1975. The psychological practitioner as a teacher: A theoretical-historical and practical review. *Counseling Psychologist* 5; 31–50.

Bandler, R., and Grinder, J. 1975. *The Structure of Magic.* Palo Alto, Ca.: Leisure and Behavior Books.

Bandura, A. 1969. *Principles of Behavior Modification.* New York: Holt, Rinehart & Winston.

Baron, R., and Liebert, R. 1971. *Human Social Behavior.* Homewood, Ill.: Dorsey Press.

Bloom, B. 1963. Definitional aspects of crisis. *J. Consulting Psychology* 27; 184–89.

Brammer, L., and Shostrom, E. 1977. *Therapeutic Psychology: An Approach to Actualization Counseling and Psychotherapy.* 3rd ed. Englewood Cliffs, N.J.: Prentice-Hall.

Bruner, J. 1972. Nature and uses of immaturity. *Amer. Psychol.* 27; 1–22.

Bullmer, K. 1972. Improving accuracy of interpersonal perception through a direct teaching method. *J. Counseling Psychology* 19; 37–41.

Caplan, Gerald. 1964. *Principles of Preventive Psychiatry.* New York: Basic Books.

CARKHUFF, R. 1968. Differential functioning of lay and professional helpers. *J. Counseling Psychology* 15; 117–26.

———. 1969. *Helping and Human Relations.* 2 vols. New York: Holt, Rinehart & Winston.

———, and BERENSON, B. 1967. *Beyond Counseling and Therapy.* New York: Holt, Rinehart & Winston.

———, and TRUAX, C. 1965. Lay mental health counseling. *J. Consulting Psychology* 29; 426–31.

CARSON, R. 1967. A and B therapist types: A critical variable in psychotherapy. *J. Nervous and Mental Disease* 144; 47–54.

COMBS, A., et al. 1969. *Florida Studies in the Helping Professions.* Gainesville: University Presses of Florida.

CORLISS, R., and RABE, P. 1969. *Psychotherapy from the Center: A Humanistic View of Change and Growth.* Scranton, Pa.: International Textbook.

CUNNINGHAM, G. 1970. Activity-oriented learning package for increasing individual counseling competencies. Spokane, Wa.: Spokane Schools TTT Project. Unpublished mimeographed manuscript.

DANISH, S. 1971. Film-simulated counselor training. *Counselor Education and Supervision* 11; 29–35.

DARBONNE, A. 1967. Crisis: A review of theory, practice and research. *Psychotherapy: Theory, Research and Practice* 4; 49–56.

DILLEY, J., LEE, J., and VERRILL, E. 1971. Is empathy ear-to-ear or face-to-face? *Personnel and Guidance J.* 50; 188–91.

DOUGHERTY, A. M., and DYAL, M. A. 1976. Community involvement: Training parents as tutors in a junior high school. *The School Counselor* 23; 353–56.

EGAN, G. 1975. *The Skilled Helper.* Monterey, Ca.: Brooks/Cole.

ELLIS, A. 1962. *Reason and Emotion in Psychotherapy.* New York: Lyle Stuart.

FRANKL, V. 1965. *The Doctor and the Soul, from Psychotherapy to Logotherapy.* 2nd ed. New York: Alfred A. Knopf.

GILLIS, J. S. 1974. Social influence therapy: The therapist as manipulator. *Psychology Today* 7; 91–95.

GOODMAN, G., and DOOLEY, D. 1976. A framework for help-intended communication. *Psychotherapy: Theory, Research and Practice* 13; 106–17.

GORDON, T. 1970. *Parent Effectiveness Training.* New York: Peter H. Wyden.

GUERNEY, B. 1969. *Psychotherapeutic Agents.* New York: Holt, Rinehart & Winston.

GURIN, G., VEROFF, J., and FELD, S. 1960. *Americans View Their Mental Health.* New York: Basic Books.

HADLEY, J., and STRUPP, H. 1976. Contemporary views of negative effects in psychotherapy. *Archives of General Psychiatry* 33; 1291–94.

HAWKINSHIRE, F. 1963. Training needs for offenders working in community treatment program. *Experiments in Culture Expansion.* Sacramento, Ca.: State Department of Corrections.

HILL, R. 1958. Generic features of families under stress. *Social Casework* 29; 32–39. Also reprinted in Parad, H. 1965. *Crisis Intervention: Selected Readings*. New York: Family Service Association of America.

HOBBS, N. 1964. Mental health's third revolution. *American J. Orthopsychiatry* 34; 822–33.

HOLMES, T., and RAHE, R. 1967. The social readjustment rating scale. *J. of Psychosomatic Research* 2; 216–18.

HOMME, L. 1971. *How to Use Contingency Contracting in the Classroom*. rev. ed. Champaign, Ill.: Research Press.

HOSFORD, R., and SORENSON, D. 1969. Participating in classroom discussions. Ch. 24 in Krumboltz, J., and Thoreson, C. 1976. *Counseling*. New York: Holt, Rinehart & Winston.

HOWARD, J. 1970. *Please Touch*. New York: McGraw-Hill.

HURVITZ, N. 1970. Peer self-help psychotherapy groups and their implications for psychotherapy. *Psychotherapy: Theory and Research* 7; 4–49.

IVEY, A. 1977. *Microcounseling: Interviewing Skills Manual*. 2nd ed. Springfield, Ill.: Charles C. Thomas.

———, and WEINSTEIN, G. 1970. The counselor as a specialist in psychological education. *Personnel and Guidance Journal* 49; 98–107.

———, et al. 1968. Micro-counseling and attending behavior. *J. Counseling Psychology* 15; Monogr. Suppl. 1–12.

JACOBSON, E. 1938. *Progressive Relaxation*. 2nd ed. Chicago: The University of Chicago Press.

JOSLIN, L. 1965. Knowledge and counseling competence. *Personnel and Guidance J.* 43; 790–95.

JUNG, C., et al. 1971. *Leader's Manual: Interpersonal Communications*. Portland, Ore.: Copy Print Center.

KAGAN, N. 1971. Influencing human interaction. East Lansing: Michigan State University CCTV. Mimeographed.

KAUL, T., and SCHMIDT, L. 1971. Dimensions of interviewer trustworthiness. *J. Counseling Psychology* 18; 542–48.

KORNER, I. 1970. Hope as a method of coping. *J. Consulting and Clinical Psychology* 34; 134–39.

KRUMBOLTZ, J. 1966. Stating the goals of counseling. Monograph 1. Fullerton, Ca.: *California Personnel and Guidance Association*.

———, and SHEPPARD, L. 1969. Vocational problem-solving experiences. Ch. 32 in Krumboltz, J., and Thoreson, C. 1976. *Counseling*. New York: Holt, Rinehart & Winston.

———, and THORESON, C. 1976. *Counseling*. New York: Holt, Rinehart & Winston.

LAZARUS, A. 1966. Behavior rehearsal vs. non-directive therapy vs. advice in effecting behavior change. *Behavior Research and Therapy* 4; 209–12.

———, 1971. Relaxation Exercises (cassette tapes, series B). Chicago: The Human Development Institute.

LEONARD, G. 1973. *The Transformation.* New York: Dell.

LIBOW, J. A., and DOTY, D. W. 1976. An evaluation of empathic listening in telephone counseling. *J. Counseling Psychology* 23; 532–37.

LINDEMANN, E. 1944. Symptomatology and management of acute grief. *American J. Psychiatry* 101; 7–21. Reprinted in Parad, H. 1965. *Crisis Intervention: Selected Readings.* New York: Family Service Association of America.

MAGOON, T. 1969. Developing skills for solving educational and vocational problems. Ch. 36 in Krumboltz, J., and Thoreson, C. 1976. *Counseling.* New York: Holt, Rinehart & Winston.

MASLOW, A. 1962. *Toward a Psychology of Being.* New York: D. Van Nostrand.

MEYER, J., STROWIG, W., and HOSFORD, R. 1970. Behavioral reinforcement with rural high school youth. *J. Counseling Psychology* 17; 127–32.

MICKELSON, D., and STEVIC, R. 1971. Differential effects of facilitative and non-facilitative behavioral counsels. *J. Counseling Psychology* 18; 314–19.

MILLER, G., and GELATT, H. Winter 1971–72. Deciding. *College Board Review* 82.

MORLEY, W., MESSICK, J., and AGUILERA, D. 1967. Crisis: Paradigms of intervention. *J. Psychiatric Nursing* 5; 537–38.

MOSHER, R. L., and SPRINTHALL, N. A. 1971. Psychological education: A means to promote personal development during adolescence. *The Counseling Psychologist* 2; 3–84.

O'LEARY, K., POULOS, R., and DEVINE, B. 1972. Tangible reinforcers: Bonuses or bribes? *J. Consulting and Clinical Psychology* 38; 1–8.

PARAD, H. 1965. *Crisis Intervention: Selected Readings.* New York: Family Service Association of America.

PERLS, F. 1969. *Gestalt Therapy Verbatim.* Lafayette, Ca.: Real People Press.

PHILLIPS, E., FIXSEN, E., and WOLF, M. 1971. *The Teaching-Family Handbook.* Lawrence, Kans.: Bureau of Child Research, Department of Human Development. Mimeographed.

PIERCE, R., and DRASGOW, J. 1969. Teaching facilitative interpersonal functioning to psychiatric inpatients. *J. Counseling Psychology* 16; 295–99.

PYLE, R., and SNYDER, F. 1971. Students as paraprofessional counselors at community colleges. *J. College Student Personnel* 12; 259–62.

REIK, T. 1948. *Listening with the Third Ear.* New York: Grove Press.

RIESSMAN, F. 1965. The helper therapy principle. *Social Work* 10; 27–32.

RIOCH, M. 1966. Changing concepts in the training of therapists. *J. Consulting Psychology* 30; 290–92.

ROGERS, C. 1951. *Client Centered Counseling.* Boston: Houghton Mifflin.

———. 1957. The necessary and sufficient conditions of therapeutic personality change. *J. Consulting Psychology* 21; 95–103.

———. 1961. *On Becoming a Person.* Boston: Houghton Mifflin.

RYAN, T., and KRUMBOLTZ, J. 1964. Effect of planned reinforcement counseling on client decision-making behavior. *J. of Counseling Psychology* 11; 315–23.

SARASON, I. 1968. Verbal learning, modeling and juvenile delinquency. *American Psychologist* 23: 254–66.

———, and GANZER, V. 1971. Modeling: an approach to the rehabilitation of juvenile offenders. Unpublished report to Department of Health, Education, and Welfare, Washington, D.C.

SCHMIDT, L., and STRONG, S. 1970. Expert and inexpert counselors. *J. Counseling Psychology* 17; 115–18.

SCHOFIELD, W. 1964. *Psychotherapy: The Purchase of Friendship.* Englewood Cliffs, N.J.: Prentice-Hall.

STEENLAND, R. 1973. Paraprofessionals in counseling centers. *Personnel and Guidance J.* 51; 417–18.

STEWART, N. 1969. Exploring and processing information about educational and vocational opportunities in groups. Ch. 26 in Krumboltz, J., and Thoreson, C. 1976. *Counseling.* New York: Holt, Rinehart & Winston.

STRONG, S. 1968. Counseling: An interpersonal influence process. *J. Counseling Psychology* 15; 215–24.

———, and SCHMIDT, L. 1970. Trustworthiness and influence in counseling. *J. Counseling Psychology* 17; 197–204.

THORESON, C. 1972. Learning House. Stanford, Ca.: Stanford University. Mimeographed.

TRUAX, C., and CARKHUFF, R. 1964. The old and the new: theory and research in counseling and psychotherapy. *Personnel and Guidance J.* 42; 860–66.

———. 1967. *Toward Effective Counseling and Psychotherapy: Training and Practice.* Chicago: Aldine.

VARENHORST, B. 1969. Learning the consequences of life's decisions. Ch. 33 in Krumboltz, J. and Thoreson, C. 1976. *Counseling.* New York: Holt, Rinehart & Winston.

———, and HAMBURG, B. 1971. Peer counselor program and curriculum. Palo Alto, Ca.: Palo Alto Unified School District. Mimeographed.

———. 1972. Progress report and current status of the Palo Alto peer counseling program. Palo Alto, Ca.: Palo Alto Unified School District, Mimeographed.

WEISSBERG, M. 1977. The curative factor in counseling and psychotherapy. *Personnel and Guidance J.* 56; 439–41.

WHITEHORN, J., and BETZ, B. 1960. Further studies of the doctor as a crucial variable in the outcome of treatment with schizophrenic patients. *American J. of Psychiatry* 117; 215–23.

WOLPE, J. 1952. Objective psychotherapy of the neuroses. *South African Medical Journal* 26; 825–29.

YABLONSKY, L. 1965. *The Travel Back: Synanon.* New York: Macmillan.

Youth in the Ghetto. 1964. New York: Harlem Youth Opportunities Unlimited.

Index